COURTING EQUALITY

COURTING

EQUALITY

A Documentary History of America's First Legal Same-Sex Marriages

Text by **PATRICIA A. GOZEMBA** and **KAREN KAHN**

Photographs by **MARILYN HUMPHRIES**

BEACON PRESS, BOSTON

Courting Equality
would not have been
possible without the
generous support of:
American Civil Liberties
Union of Massachusetts,
Karen Rudolph and Jimi
Simmons, and Wainwright Bank

BEACON PRESS
25 Beacon Street
Boston, Massachusetts 02108-2892
www.beacon.org

Beacon Press books
are published under the auspices of
the Unitarian Universalist Association of Congregations.

09 08 07 8 7 6 5 4 3 2 1

This book is printed on acid-free paper that meets the uncoated paper ANSI/NISO
specifications for permanence as revised in 1992.

Text design by Patricia Duque Campos

Library of Congress Cataloging-in-Publication Data

Gozemba, Patricia A.
  Courting equality : a documentary history of same-sex marriage in America / text by
Patricia A. Gozemba and Karen Kahn ; photographs by Marilyn Humphries.
      p. cm.
  Includes bibliographical references.
  ISBN-13: 978-0-8070-6620-1 (hardcover : alk. paper)
  ISBN-10: 0-8070-6620-6 (hardcover : alk. paper) 1. Same-sex marriage-United States.
  2.Same-sex marriage-Law and legislation-United States. 3. Gay rights-United States.
  I. Kahn, Karen II. Title. HQ1034.U5G69 2007
  306.84'80973-dc22   2006031579

For the *Goodridge* Plaintiffs:

Hillary and Julie Goodridge

David Wilson and Robert Compton

Gloria Bailey and Linda Davies

Gary Chalmers and Rich Linnell

Heidi and Gina Nortonsmith

Maureen Brodoff and Ellen Wade

Mike Horgan and Ed Balmelli

YOU HAVE RAISED OUR HOPES FOR JUSTICE AND EQUALITY.
May your example inspire our people all across this country to achieve full civil rights.

CONTENTS

PHOTOGRAPHER'S PREFACE

The same-sex marriage movement crept up on me, as I think it did with many people. One day it was a part of the gay and lesbian movement, and then suddenly, at least in Massachusetts, it was the public face of the gay and lesbian movement. November 18, 2003, the day of the *Goodridge* decision, felt like a starter's gun signaling the beginning of so many people's efforts to keep same-sex marriage legal in this state. For me it meant a calendar full of events and deadlines related to these efforts.

Many of the photographs in *Courting Equality* were the result of assignments from *Gay Community News* 1983-1992 and *Bay Windows* 1992 to the present, newspapers for which I have been a freelance contributor. It was and is an honor to collaborate with the dedicated staff of these newspapers who have worked so tirelessly to cover the LGBT (lesbian, gay, bisexual, and transgender) community.

Of all the events that stand out for me, the most compelling were the four days of the constitutional conventions at the Massachusetts State House, February 11 and 12 and March 11 and 29, 2004. My day began at 6 a.m. and often ended after midnight, and I was not alone.

In addition to the legislators and lobbyists on both sides of the marriage equality issue, there were the thousands of citizens of Massachusetts (and other states) who stayed at the State House sometimes for twelve to fourteen hours a day. Those days are etched in my memory, and I can still see and hear the crowd standing in the roped-off corridor facing the house chambers, singing and chanting from the beginning to the end of the day. Throughout those days I never for a moment forgot the importance of the democratic process that was being played out in front of me and what a privilege it was to be there documenting it.

My hope is that the photographs in this book will help others understand what went on in Massachusetts, how so many people, heterosexual and LGBT alike, fought for an issue that conferred the dignity as well as the benefits of marriage to the gay and lesbian community.

I believe that when others look at the faces of these families and the people who worked so hard in this struggle they will see the same compelling combination of hope and dignity that I do and will understand our commonality and responsibility to one another.

Marilyn Humphries

ABBREVIATIONS

ACLU	American Civil Liberties Union
DSS	Department of Social Services
DOMA	Defense of Marriage Act
FTMC	Freedom to Marry Coalition
GLAD	Gay & Lesbian Advocates & Defenders
HRC	Human Rights Campaign
LGBT	Lesbian, Gay, Bisexual and Transgender
MCC	Metropolitan Community Church
MFI	Massachusetts Family Institute
MGLPC	Massachusetts Gay and Lesbian Political Caucus
NGLTF	National Gay and Lesbian Task Force
RCFM	Religious Coalition for the Freedom to Marry
SEIU	Service Employees International Union
SJC	Supreme Judicial Court

The seven plaintiff couples in *Goodridge v. Department of Public Health* gathered on March 12, 2002 outside Suffolk Superior Court House, where their case was argued by GLAD attorney Jennifer Levi. Pictured, first row (L-R): Gary Chalmers and Rich Linnell; Ellen Wade and Maureen Brodoff; Gloria Bailey and Linda Davies. Second row (L-R): Mike Horgan and Ed Balmelli; David Wilson and Rob Compton; Heidi Norton and Gina Smith; and Hillary and Julie Goodridge.

INTRODUCTION

*It is impossible to pretend that being denied the right to marry
the person of your choice is anything but a massive affront to
the human dignity and equality of LGBT [lesbian, gay, bisexual,
and transgender] people in a culture where that choice is cherished
as a fundamental freedom essential to the pursuit of happiness.*

—*Mary Bonauto*, Harvard Civil Rights–Civil Liberties Law Review

THE STAGE IS SET

Mary Bonauto, a young lawyer just over five feet tall but with steely determination in her deep blue eyes, hated to say "No" to a just cause. When she joined New England's Gay & Lesbian Advocates & Defenders (GLAD) legal team in March 1990, however, she turned down multiple requests by same-sex couples to sue for the right to marry. She didn't believe she could win, and she wasn't going to start that fight until she could.

It wasn't that Bonauto didn't understand the importance of marriage to gay families. Prior to coming to GLAD, she had practiced law in Portland, Maine, during the height of the AIDS epidemic. She felt deep anguish each time she received a call from a pay phone made by a man who had just lost his longtime partner and then been barred from his home by his partner's so-called family. These experiences, she says, were "searing for me as a young attorney, and they brought into sharp relief the need for family protections for our community."

Nonetheless, during her early years at GLAD, Bonauto remained patient and deliberate. Winning the right to civil marriage for same-sex couples would take careful planning; the foundation would have to be laid "brick by brick," using all the tactics available to the gay and lesbian community: public education, political activism, and the right legal challenges. Bonauto believed that until the public and the legal system could see gay men and lesbians as whole people, with the same aspirations and needs as others, no court would grant marriage rights to same-sex couples. And when you lose in court, she says, "you establish a precedent that sticks with you for twenty to twenty-five years."

It was ten years before Bonauto and her colleagues decided that GLAD and its allies had built the solid foundation needed to challenge Massachusetts marriage laws. By then, GLAD had successfully challenged discrimination against gay men and lesbians in several critical court battles, including Vermont's civil-marriage suit. Bonauto selected seven Massachusetts couples and asked them each to request a marriage license at their local city or town hall. The licenses were all denied. On April 11, 2001, GLAD filed a lawsuit—*Goodridge v. Department of Public Health*—on their behalf.

THE *GOODRIDGE* DECISION

As GLAD explained in its legal brief, largely authored by Bonauto, the seven couples wished to marry for the same reasons as heterosexual couples: to symbolize their love and commitment; to protect their families in times of crisis; to access benefits such as family health insurance, hospital visitation rights, and joint property rights; to give their children greater security; and to proclaim to their communities their status as families. Their goal was not to undermine marriage, as those opposed to same-sex marriage contended, but to solidify their familial relations by participating in one of society's most sacred institutions.

The plaintiff couples included Hillary and Julie Goodridge, Ellen Wade and Maureen Brodoff, Linda Davies and Gloria Bailey, Rob Compton and

Dave Wilson, Heidi Norton and Gina Smith, Mike Horgan and Ed Balmelli, and Gary Chalmers and Richard Linnell. Spread across the state in rural, suburban, and urban communities, the couples had been together anywhere from five to thirty years. Four of the couples were raising children together. Several had experienced major health crises. All were active members of their communities, participating in religious congregations, PTAs, sports teams, and neighborhood organizations. In choosing these seven couples from the dozens who were willing to sacrifice their privacy in order to challenge Massachusetts marriage laws, the GLAD team sought those who would make the best public educators. What was most important, Bonauto said, was that each of the plaintiffs could "speak from the heart with authenticity and conviction about why marriage mattered to them."

When the Suffolk Superior Court ruled against the plaintiff couples in May 2002, the GLAD attorneys appealed directly to the Massachusetts Supreme Judicial Court (SJC). Oral arguments were heard March 4, 2003. Bonauto argued that "the right to marry a person of one's own choice is protected under the equal liberty and due process protections of the Massachusetts State Constitution." She noted that the court had a history of "respect for private personal decisions and expressive and intimate associations." The state argued that marriage must remain a heterosexual institution for four reasons: (1) procreation is the fundamental purpose of marriage, (2) families with mothers and fathers are better for children, (3) the legislature, not the courts, should be responsible for changing marriage statutes, and (4) extending benefits to same-sex couples would be costly to the state.

Bonauto successfully demolished each of the state's arguments. Championing the civil rights of gay and lesbian people, she won. On November 18, 2003, in a 4–3 decision, the SJC ruled that:

The Massachusetts Constitution affirms the dignity and equality of all individuals. It forbids the creation of second-class citizens. In reaching our conclusion we have given full deference to the arguments made by

"It was in Massachusetts, our nation's "Cradle of Liberty," that slavery was first abolished in a court decision, *Jennison v. Caldwell,* in 1783. How fitting that in 2003, it was again in Massachusetts that a court decision, *Goodridge v. Department of Public Health,* became the first to abolish sex discrimination in marriage."

—*Evan Wolfson*, Why Marriage Matters

the Commonwealth. But it has failed to identify any constitutionally adequate reason for denying civil marriage to same-sex couples.

The justices ordered the state to begin issuing marriage licenses to same-sex couples on May 17, 2004, the fiftieth anniversary of one of the greatest civil rights cases of the twentieth century, *Brown v. the Board of Education*. The unintended symmetry was not lost on gay men and lesbians, who had been fighting to overcome their second-class citizenship for more than half a century.

THE IMPACT

Goodridge shook the nation. By clearly stating that marriage was not defined by opposite-sex partnerships, the decision exacerbated an already bitter cultural divide between religious conservatives and those who believe that secular values underlie America's constitutional liberties. In reaction, a flurry of states proposed legislation to prevent same-sex marriage. At the same time, a few municipal officials challenged state laws by issuing marriage licenses to same-sex couples in their cities and counties. Throughout the winter and spring of 2004, same-sex marriage became a rolling act of civil disobedience. First Gavin Newsom, the mayor of San Francisco, and then officials in cities as diverse as Asbury Park, New Jersey; New Paltz, New York; Portland, Oregon; and Sandoval County, New Mexico, began allowing same-sex couples to marry. All of these marriages were eventually declared illegal by state courts. In Massachusetts, however, multiple legislative and legal challenges to the *Goodridge* decision were defeated. As a result, marriage for same-sex couples became a reality on May 17, 2004, as the court had ordered.

While marriage equality supporters celebrated victory—and same-sex couples began planning their long-awaited weddings—religious and social conservatives prepared to fight back. They planned to make the fall presidential election a referendum on the rights of gay men and lesbians. On November 2, 2004, voters in eleven states passed constitutional bans on same-sex marriage. In several cases, these amendments went far beyond simply banning marriage; they also barred same-sex couples from entering into domestic partnerships or any other contractual relationship that could confer benefits similar to those granted married spouses.

Democrats, who had nominated Massachusetts senator John Kerry as their presidential candidate, questioned whether the *Goodridge* decision—and the related ballot questions—aided George Bush's electoral victory. Right-wing pundits said that once again Massachusetts liberals had put fear into the heart of middle America. The nation, they claimed, wasn't ready for gay marriage.

During this frenetic national showdown, however, a different and more complex story was emerging in Massachusetts. That story, both political and personal, is the subject of this book. The *Goodridge* decision provoked a searing public debate in the commonwealth over the meaning of marriage and family, civil rights, and the role of religion in law and society. The decision also positively changed the lives of thousands of families, providing them with a new level of legal and emotional security.

DEBATING FAMILY VALUES

Conservatives insist that marriage is a religious institution that has gone unchanged for three thousand years, but marriage and family have long been sites of cultural conflict. It is through marriage and family that we establish our most intimate relationships, pass on values, and reproduce our social order. The central role marriage plays in our lives makes it a particularly contentious issue during times of social upheaval.

Over the last forty years, Americans have been embroiled in a cultural firestorm over marriage and family, or what has come to be called "family values." These debates, which encompass a range of social issues from abortion to gay rights to women's roles in the family and workplace, have also become a struggle over the role of conservative religious values in American society. Catholic and fundamentalist Protestant churches have led the opposition to gay and lesbian civil rights on the grounds that homosexuality is a religious sin. They argue that same-sex marriage will destroy a sacred religious institution. These religious activists don't acknowledge that civil marriage is a secular institution through which the state grants multiple financial and social benefits to family units. It is, after all, not the religious ceremony of marriage but the state license that makes a marriage legal under federal and state law. In the United States, nearly 40 percent of marriages are performed without any religious ceremony at all.

Feminist and Gay Liberation Movements Question Marriage and Family
Today's family values debates began with the feminist and gay liberation movements of the sixties and seventies. These movements challenged sex-role stereotypes, limits on sexual freedom, and the male-dominated nuclear family. Even within these movements, however, ideological conflicts arose over whether marriage and the nuclear family should be replaced with new forms of intimacy and community or whether these institutions could be reformed in ways that would allow for greater equality.

Declaring "the personal is political," feminists popularized consciousness-raising groups, in which women analyzed their daily experiences as wives, mothers, and daughters. Some rejected marriage and family, feeling it was the root cause of their oppression, while others sought equality within marriage. They used the legislative and legal arenas to dismantle sexist language in marriage statutes, press for no-fault divorce, and ensure joint custody arrangements for children. Capitalizing on medical advances, feminists also used the courts to give women greater control over their decisions regarding motherhood. These changes increased women's sexual and economic autonomy, making marriage a more equal partnership by law but leaving men and women to struggle over what this new equality would look like in reality.

In the 1970s, gay activists fought to end an array of discriminatory practices that limited employment opportunities, housing options, and sexual expression, and that quietly sanctioned violent attacks on people who did not conform to traditional gender roles. Movement leaders, however, had little interest in promoting marriage, which they saw as an oppressive institution that reinforced the very gender stereotypes gay liberation hoped to eliminate.

Same-Sex Couples Challenge Their Exclusion from Marriage

Most lesbians and gay men, though, were not activists. They lived quietly in small towns and cities scattered across America, and they yearned for full legal and social validation of their relationships. Recognizing the desire of many same-sex couples to join in committed unions, blessed by God and their communities, the Reverend Troy Perry made "holy unions" a central part of the mission of his gay evangelical Metropolitan Community Church (MCC). Since the church's founding in 1968, thousands of same-sex couples have participated in MCC and other religious ceremonies sanctifying their unions. Others have created their own commitment ceremonies to honor their relationships with family and friends.

Empowered by the newly emerging gay liberation movement, a few gay men and lesbians were determined to challenge their exclusion from civil marriage. On May 18, 1970, one such couple, Richard (Jack) Baker and James M. McConnell of Minnesota, held a press conference announcing their plan to marry. Then they headed to the city clerk's office.

The Minneapolis city clerk who took Baker and McConnell's application sought an opinion from the county attorney, who argued that issuing the two men a marriage license would "result in an undermining and destruction of the entire legal concept of our family structure in all areas of law." When refused a license, the couple sued; their case, along with numerous others in the 1970s, was dismissed on the grounds that marriage was by definition a heterosexual union.

In the early seventies, stories like McConnell and Baker's, along with feminist challenges to traditional gender roles and real changes in the structure of American families—the 1970 census showed that the majority of Americans no longer lived in traditional nuclear families—contributed to a growing sense of anxiety among conservatives. Media headlines decried the decline of the family and the rise of the sexual revolution. Many Americans, but especially fundamentalist and evangelical Christians, were not ready for a society in which gender roles were more fluid, women more independent, and family structures more diverse.

Religious Conservatives Defend the "Traditional" Family

These social changes provoked a conservative backlash. For more than three decades, the religious right has fiercely defended its vision of the traditional American family, with its male head of household, subservient wife, and obedient children, as the cornerstone of a moral society. Notably, long before gay and lesbian movement leaders embraced marriage as a goal, religious conservatives rallied against it. They saw same-sex marriage as a radical challenge to biblical teachings and the strict gender roles that ordered their day-to-day lives.

Fears of a world in which male and female roles were no longer clearly defined—symbolized by hot-button issues like same-sex marriage, abortion rights, and working moms and stay-at-home dads—built the infrastructure for a conservative movement that has had considerable success since the 1970s. In 2006, forty-six states and the federal government defined civil marriage as "the union of one man and one woman," a definition firmly rooted in religious values rather than constitutional principles of liberty and equality. Yet while conservatives continue to win skirmishes on the battlefield, their war has already been lost. Women are not going back to hearth and home, and gay men and lesbians are not returning to the closet.

COMING OUT—A NEW OPENNESS CHALLENGES STEREOTYPES AND DISCRIMINATION

Nationally, anti-gay sentiment peaked in 1987, with 78 percent of Americans claiming that homosexual relations were always wrong. By 2002, a Gallup poll showed that less than 50 percent of Americans thought homosexuality was an unacceptable alternative lifestyle, while 86 percent believed that gay men and lesbians should have equal rights in employment.

The biggest factor in this remarkable sea change in attitude had been the individual decisions by millions of gay men and lesbians to come out—that is, to openly identify themselves to family, friends, and colleagues. In 1985, only one quarter of Americans reported that friends, relatives, or coworkers had told them they were gay, and more than half believed they didn't know any gay people. By 2000, 75 percent of the population reported knowing someone gay, and 56 percent reported having a gay friend or close acquaintance. Moreover, young people, exposed through popular culture to gay people and gay themes (from Ellen DeGeneres to *Will and Grace* to *Brokeback Mountain*), increasingly reject the homophobia of earlier generations.

This new cultural acceptance of homosexuality was brought home on June 26, 2003, when the U.S. Supreme Court reversed its 1986 *Bowers v. Hardwick* decision in *Lawrence v. Texas*. *Bowers*, in upholding a Georgia sodomy law, asserted that the federal Constitution did not protect homosexual sex. *Lawrence* involved a similar consensual, private sexual encounter, but this time the Court reached the opposite conclusion, declaring that "when homosexual conduct is made criminal by the law of the State, that declaration in and of itself is an invitation to subject homosexual persons to discrimination both in the public and private spheres." For the first time, the highest court in the nation saw gay men and lesbians as whole human beings whose sexual orientation could not be used to diminish their humanity.

Though *Lawrence* did not concern the issue of gay marriage, in his dissent Justice Scalia, carrying the banner for the conservative movement, lamented that *Lawrence* would open the door for same-sex marriage. Unlike the 1970s, when conservative fears of gay marriage were far ahead of the gay liberation movement's embrace of the cause, by 2003 equal marriage rights had moved to the top of the gay and lesbian civil rights agenda. Though equal marriage is not the final frontier for ensuring equality and justice for all lesbian, gay, bisexual, and transgender people, ending marriage discrimination has

*W*hen homosexual
conduct is made criminal
by the law of the State, that
declaration in and of itself
is an invitation to subject
homosexual persons to
discrimination both in the
public and private spheres. . . .
The petitioners are entitled to
respect for their private lives.
The State cannot demean
their existence or control their
destiny by making their private sexual conduct a crime.
Their right to liberty under the
Due Process Clause gives them
the full right to engage in their
conduct without intervention
of the government.

—*U.S. Supreme Court majority opinion,*
Lawrence v. Texas

become an attainable goal with the potential of tangible benefits for thousands of families.

A MOVEMENT FOR MARRIAGE EQUALITY

Although many same-sex couples longed to marry, the possibility seemed so
remote before the 1990s that lesbian and gay civil rights groups simply
refused to entertain the issue. At the beginning of that decade, only two
states—Wisconsin and Massachusetts—had antidiscrimination laws that
protected gay men and lesbians from being fired from their jobs or refused
housing because of their sexual orientation. Legal recognition of same-sex
relationships was even more limited, with family law courts often ruling
against gay men and lesbians. In a particularly notorious case in the mid-
eighties, Karen Thompson had to fight her partner Sharon Kowalski's parents
for years to gain guardianship of—and make medical decisions for—Sharon,
who had been severely injured in a car accident. Seeing that kind of vulnera-
bility made lesbians and gay men acutely aware of the need for legal recognition of their relationships, but it also made civil marriage seem more like a
pipe dream than a real possibility.

In 1993, that pipe dream suddenly appeared to be within reach. In a civil-
marriage suit brought by three same-sex couples, the Hawaii Supreme Court
ruled that the refusal to grant marriage licenses to same-sex couples violated
the state's equal rights amendment. Evan Wolfson, co-counsel in the case and
the visionary leader of the marriage equality movement, began a nationwide
tour urging gay organizations to join the fight for civil marriage.

Gay men and lesbians never won the right to marry in Hawaii. The state
supreme court sent the case back to the trial court, asking the state to present a "compelling reason" for denying marriage licenses to the plaintiff couples. As the case dragged on, religious conservatives poured money into Hawaii in support of a state constitutional amendment that would essentially
ban same-sex marriage. The amendment passed in 1998.

LGBT people and their allies rallied at Copley Square in Boston on June 26, 2003, to celebrate the Supreme Court ruling in *Lawrence v. Texas*.

In the meantime, Wolfson's marriage campaign caught on in Vermont. In 1995, local activists formed the Freedom to Marry Task Force. Two years later, the two attorneys who had founded the group, Susan Murray and Beth Robinson, along with Mary Bonauto from GLAD, filed a lawsuit on behalf of three plaintiff couples.

Bonauto had become increasingly committed to ending the exclusion of gay men and lesbians from marriage. Having won a number of adoption and custody cases in Massachusetts that established gay families as legitimate in the eyes of the law—and having seen the benefits and limitations of domestic-partnership laws—she was convinced that marriage was the legal scheme that best protected families. She explained, "I felt like our litigation options were limited. With most of the rights of marriage, there's an explicit rule, that the benefit, protection, or responsibility is available to a 'spouse.' And in the end the only way we'd be able to end the denial of those protections would be to become spouses."

In 1999, Vermont's supreme court declared in *Baker v. the State of Vermont* that the state's marriage laws discriminated against same-sex couples. Much to the lawyers' dismay, however, the court did not order the state to begin issuing marriage licenses to same-sex couples. Instead, the court left it to the legislature to find a remedy. The inventive legislative solution was *civil unions*, a state-sanctioned partnership that offers the rights and benefits of marriage granted by the state of Vermont but lacks legal standing anywhere else in the country.

With such near victories in Hawaii and Vermont, gay and lesbian civil rights organizations could no longer ignore the groundswell of grassroots support for marriage equality. Wolfson founded the National Freedom to Marry Coalition, and national organizations such as the Human Rights Campaign and National Gay and Lesbian Task Force began to put their muscle behind the marriage cause. By the time GLAD filed the *Goodridge* lawsuit in Massachusetts, on April 11, 2001, the movement for marriage equality was picking up speed around the world.

The Netherlands legalized same-sex marriage on April 1, 2001, followed by Belgium and the Canadian provinces of Ontario and British Columbia in 2003. By 2006, same-sex marriage was the law of the land throughout Canada, much of Europe, and South Africa. When the SJC ruled in favor of the plaintiff couples in November 2003, Massachusetts was hardly alone in having recognized that choosing one's marriage partner is a fundamental civil right.

A STRONG LEGAL FOUNDATION

Though controversial, the majority opinion in *Goodridge* was built on a strong foundation of federal and state court rulings. Those rulings recognized individual rights to privacy in intimate relations and acknowledged that choosing one's marriage partner is an essential part of exercising one's freedom as a human being.

In 1948, the California high court, reversing the state's interracial marriage ban, declared in *Perez v. Sharp* that marriage is "one of the basic civil rights of man." The majority opinion continued: "The right to marry is the right to join in marriage with the person of one's choice." In 1967, the U.S. Supreme Court agreed, asserting in *Loving v. Virginia*, "Marriage is one of the 'basic civil rights of man,' fundamental to our very existence and survival." In overturning all remaining antimiscegenation laws, the Court emphasized that under the U.S. Constitution, "the freedom to marry, or not marry, a person of another race resides with the individual and cannot be infringed by the State."

The SJC's *Goodridge* decision drew on these and subsequent marriage cases, as well as on numerous federal and state precedents regarding rights to privacy in intimate and familial relations. Since the 1960s, key U.S. Supreme Court decisions have clarified that the Constitution protects "personal decisions relating to marriage, procreation, contraception, family relationships, child rearing, and education." Citing the U.S. Supreme Court's most recent decision in this arena, *Lawrence v. Texas* (June 2003), the SJC concluded that under the U.S. Constitution "the core concept of common human dignity . . .

precludes government intrusion into the deeply personal realms of consensual adult expressions of intimacy and one's choice of an intimate partner."

Throughout its 225-year history, the Massachusetts constitution, written by John Adams, has been interpreted to provide broader liberty protections than the U.S. Constitution. In 1783, for instance, long before the nation entered into a civil war over slavery, the Massachusetts Supreme Judicial Court interpreted the state constitution's Declaration of Rights to include the freedom of African Americans. Chief Justice Marshall put the *Goodridge* decision squarely within this long history of the protection of individual liberty:

> The individual liberty and equality safeguards of the Massachusetts Constitution protect both "freedom from" unwarranted government intrusion into protected spheres of life and "freedom to" partake in benefits created by the State for the common good. Whether and whom to marry, how to express sexual intimacy, and whether and how to establish a family—these are among the most basic of every individual's liberty and due process rights. . . . The liberty interest in choosing whether and whom to marry would be hollow if the Commonwealth could, without sufficient justification, foreclose an individual from freely choosing the person with whom to share an exclusive commitment in the unique institution of civil marriage.

As Marshall neatly argued, the only difference between the *Perez* and *Loving* cases and the *Goodridge* case is that the first two cases concerned the race of the marital partners and the third, the gender. The *Goodridge* plaintiffs were being excluded from civil marriage due to one single trait: their sexual orientation. The court concluded that the marriage ban appeared to be based wholly on moral judgments about homosexuality—an insufficient reason for denying an entire class of individuals their basic civil rights.

COURTING EQUALITY

Evan Wolfson has said, in explaining the importance of the struggle for equal marriage rights, that marriage provides "a vocabulary in which non-gay people talk about larger important questions—questions of love and commiment and dedication and self-sacrifice and family, but also equality and participation and connectedness. . . . In claiming that vocabulary we make it easier for non-gay people to understand who we are." The public debate in Massachusetts following the *Goodridge* decision proved Wolfson absolutely right.

In Massachusetts, the SJC's decision was greeted with the same cheers and fears exhibited toward gay marriage throughout the country. Polls taken on November 23, 2003, just five days after the court's ruling, showed the state's residents divided: 50 percent supported civil marriage for same-sex couples, while 38 percent opposed the court's decision. Though same-sex marriage supporters outnumbered those opposed, the national significance of the issue ensured that local grassroots opposition would be bolstered by national conservative organizations. Lou Sheldon of the Traditional Values Coalition announced, "Massachusetts is our Iwo Jima." The Catholic Church, a key political player in a predominantly Catholic state, vocally opposed same-sex marriage and planned to use its influence to ensure its defeat.

With the court granting a six-month stay of its decision in order to allow the legislature time to adjust the marriage statutes, a political battle was bound to ensue. The opposition immediately pursued multiple legal and legislative strategies to stop same-sex weddings from taking place as scheduled on May 17, 2004. When their efforts failed, the tenor of the debate began to change. The idea of same-sex marriage had been much more threatening than the reality.

When the legislature met in a joint session in September 2005 to reconsider an amendment to the state constitution denying full marriage equality to same-sex couples, Representative Byron Rushing wryly noted that thou-

sands of gay men and lesbians had married but Massachusetts residents none-theless walked out of their homes and found that "the sun still rose; they opened their refrigerators, and the milk hadn't curdled." Same-sex marriage had had no discernible impact on the health and welfare of Massachusetts families, except that those who had once been excluded from civil marriage could now enjoy its benefits. In a remarkable victory for marriage equality, in 2005, and again in 2006, the legislature rejected writing marriage discrimination into the Massachusetts constitution. Nonetheless, same-sex marriage opponents continued their efforts to deny full equality to Massachusetts's gay and lesbian citizens.

With a visually stunning and emotionally powerful collection of photographs, *Courting Equality* takes readers through the volatile public debate following the *Goodridge* decision and introduces some of the many lesbian and gay families who have taken advantage of the commonwealth's equal marriage laws. In Massachusetts, equal marriage has not destroyed the family but rather has reinforced the importance of love and commitment and fairness and equality to the functioning of healthy, democratic communities.

Are some families more deserving than others? Representative David Linsky, in extraordinarily moving testimony at the 2004 constitutional convention, challenged his colleagues and the citizens of the commonwealth to consider that question:

> I am the suburban dad. . . . I coach baseball, basketball, and I take my kids to football practice. . . . I know my kids' friends and their parents. I carpool them, go to Cub Scout meetings, and look out for each and every one of them like they were my own kids. The kids have sleep-overs, attend birthday parties, and go bowling. . . . When I thought about it, I realized that not all of these families were the same as mine. . . .
>
> One of those kids [with two moms] is probably the oldest and closest friend of one of my sons. There is a lot of love in that house, prob-

ably more than in most houses of married couples. That boy has been in my house nearly as much as my own kids and my kids have been welcomed at his house. I coached that boy in baseball last summer and he is a very promising catcher.

So my question is: How can I tell that boy, who has been in my house so many times, that his family isn't as good as mine? . . . How can we tell him that someone in his family shouldn't get the same benefits and responsibilities as my family or your families or anyone else's families? Please tell me how we should tell him that.

Massachusetts, by granting equal rights to all families, has found its answer—now so must the rest of the nation.

OURTING EQUALITY

Mary Bonauto outside the courthouse, learning the outcome of the case.

DIGNITY AND EQUALITY FOR ALL

The Goodridge Decision

*The Court declared that our time had come, that gay
people are now part of "we the people."*

> —*Mary Bonauto, lead attorney for the plaintiffs*, Goodridge v. Department of Public Health

AWAITING THE DECISION

The New England fall inched toward winter; *Goodridge v. Department of Public Health* should already have been decided. July 13, 2003, was the internal date that the Massachusetts Supreme Judicial Court (SJC) had set for the ruling, but on that summer day an announcement had come that the court was postponing its ruling. Speculation gathered on both sides of the same-sex marriage equality case. Each day seemed to bring more outlandish theorizing, increasing jitters, and even some wagering. Much was at stake for thousands of gay men and lesbians in the commonwealth. On October 23, 2003, after years of having their families ignored by the legislature, the lesbian and gay community watched the legislature's Joint Committee on the Judiciary hold its first-ever hearing on a same-sex marriage bill. Even without a decision, the *Goodridge* case was changing the course of history.

When GLAD attorney Mary Bonauto decided to sue for same-sex marriage rights in Massachusetts, the courts were the only option. Speaker of the House Thomas Finneran had held up action on domestic partnership and other family protection measures for years. Still, many insisted that the legislature, not the courts, should decide such a significant change in social policy. But in Vermont, when the courts had left the decision to the legislature, the result was an alternative marriage system for same-sex couples—civil unions—which was not what the gay and lesbian community of Massachusetts wanted.

Hoping to avoid Vermont's "separate but equal" outcome in Massachusetts, Bonauto had carefully answered the justices' questions in oral arguments eight months earlier, on March 4, 2003. When asked whether marriage laws should be decided by the legislature, she had replied, "We are simply asking this court to engage in a very familiar process, which is reviewing a statute and deciding whether or not that statute transgresses constitutional limitations. State courts and federal courts both have reviewed limitations on marriage having to do with race, having to do with poverty, having to do with incarceration." Stonewalled by the legislature, like many other minority groups before them, the gay and lesbian community turned to the courts to enforce their rights.

Plaintiff Rob Compton was so determined to be at the press conference announcing the court's decision that he postponed his hip surgery for three months. Shortly after 8 a.m. every day, the GLAD legal team and its allies checked the SJC Web site. Everyone knew that was the time that the court announced the cases that had been decided; they released the rulings to the public two hours later.

DECISION DAY

Finally, at 8 a.m. on November 18, 2003, the announcement came: *Goodridge* had been decided. At 10 a.m., Mary Bonauto took the short walk from her office to the court. Inside the courthouse a frenetic crowd of reporters and TV camerapeople cast about for a story. No one recognized Bonauto as the lead attorney from GLAD as she quietly picked up her printed copy of the decision. Alone, she stood on the granite steps outside the building and quickly scanned the decision. It was only then that she realized she had prevailed. Without talking to reporters, she headed back to her office. On the way, she called her parents and told them, "Fasten your seat belts."

Before knowing the decision, staff members at GLAD started calling the seven plaintiff couples. Win or lose, they had to come immediately to the GLAD offices to prepare for a quickly scheduled noon press conference at Boston's Omni Parker House Hotel. And so the families began their journeys.

Gina and Heidi

In Northampton, in the western part of the state, Gina Smith, Heidi Norton, and their two children—Avery, seven, and Quinn, four—piled into their seven-year-old station wagon and headed east on the Massachusetts Turnpike. The kids got their parents to promise them a cake—whatever the outcome. The family tuned in Northampton's WRSI FM and heard local gay-bookstore owner Mark Carmien reading the first paragraph of the decision. When he finished, they still weren't quite sure whether they had won or lost. Then Carmien and the host of the show began singing "Going to the Chapel," and Heidi and Gina got it. They and the kids broke out screaming, high-fiving, slapping the dashboard, and hitting the ceiling in ecstasy. Heidi, overcome by her own excitement, kept asking Gina, "Are you okay to drive?" Gina drove on to Boston.

he Massachusetts Constitution affirms the dignity and equality of all individuals. It forbids the creation of second-class citizens.

—*Massachusetts Supreme Judicial Court majority opinion*, Goodridge v. Department of Public Health

The Nortonsmiths, Heidi, Quinn, Avery, and Gina, all enthusiastic cyclists, love the bike trail at the end of their street in Northampton.

Gary and Rich

In the central Massachusetts town of Whitinsville, Gary Chalmers and Rich Linnell also got on the Pike and headed for Boston. Chalmers recalls that they tuned in the radio and "caught the tail end of a story that sounded positive, but we weren't sure. I called my parents, and my dad, who had been watching the story unfold on TV, said, 'You won.' We were all totally excited."

Without the right to marry—or more properly, the right to choose to marry—one is excluded from the full range of human experience and denied full protection of the laws for one's "avowed commitment to an intimate and lasting human relationship."

—*Massachusetts Supreme Judicial Court majority opinion,*
Goodridge v. Department of Public Health

Gary Chalmers and Rich Linnell
pose with their daughter, Paige,
at the foot of a tree house
that they built for her.

Plaintiffs Gloria Bailey and Linda Davies relax
on their powerboat, the *Glory B.*

Gloria and Linda

As they had every Tuesday since the waiting began, Gloria Bailey and Linda Davies left their home in Orleans on Cape Cod and headed with their cats and their press conference clothes toward their therapy practice in Hartford, Connecticut. Following their custom, when they reached the Cape Cod Canal at 8 a.m., they stopped and called the GLAD offices to see if the decision had come down. The number was busy. Busy. Strange, but . . . After ten minutes of trying to get through, they set out for Hartford on Route 495 and called friends on their cell phone to learn if the court had ruled. Well into their trip, they got the word: Get up to Boston. Back at the canal, they ran into a Burger King, changed into their press conference clothes, and had a friend pick up their cats. On the road to Boston they heard that they had won. Gloria burst into tears, and as soon as she composed herself, Linda proposed.

*T*he SJC ruling offers a vision of society in which no person is marginalized. It is a vision worth realizing.

—*Editors of the* Boston Globe

Ellen and Maureen

Maureen Brodoff, on business in Reno, was the only plaintiff fated to be out of state on the big day. Her partner, Ellen Wade, got the call from GLAD in their Newton home, just a few miles west of Boston. Months ago Ellen had given up looking at the SJC Web site every day, but when she picked up the phone just after 8 a.m. and heard GLAD's Gary Buseck on the phone, she knew what it meant. It was 6 a.m. in Reno, too early to awaken Maureen. On the drive into Boston, Ellen called Maureen, who still laughs at the irony of being in a hotel with a casino and, right next to the slot machines, a wedding chapel.

*H*ow extraordinary that a historic leap forward for human rights would involve validating our deepest love! Nothing could make us feel more joyful than that.

—*Betsy and Gail Leondar-Wright*

Kate Brodoff and her mothers, Maureen Brodoff and Ellen Wade, relax with Diana and Joey.

Hillary and Julie

For the three couples who lived in the Jamaica Plain area of Boston—Julie and Hillary Goodridge, Ed Balmelli and Mike Horgan, and Dave Wilson and Rob Compton—the trip posed fewer commuting challenges but just as much drama. The Goodridges got the call to come to the GLAD office just as Julie was leaving the house to take their seven-year-old daughter, Annie, to school. When Julie returned a half hour later, she found Hillary still in her pajamas and totally flummoxed. The jammed SJC Web site offered no help, but finally a friend called and told them that they had won. They headed for Annie's school to share the news.

*T*o me [the Goodridges] are the very definition of courage. They have put themselves out there in name, in action, and in the face of near unprecedented controversy to be recognized in the way that they feel they deserve, knowing what they were doing would be unpopular and unthinkable to many.

—*Rep. Rachel Kaprielian*

Hillary, Annie, and Julie Goodridge

Mike and Ed

Mike Horgan got the call and went into a nervous, excited panic. "I think I was about three feet off the ground. I'm running around the house doing half measures getting dressed; I found my belt, I put it down somewhere, I had no idea where I put it—that kind of thing. I was just completely out of my mind. I had to sit down and just calm down for a minute and just put things in perspective." Walking toward the GLAD offices just after 10 a.m., Horgan and Balmelli didn't know of their victory until they met Bonauto in the street. Balmelli recalls, "Mary Bonauto comes down the street, she's got the phone in her ear and she looks up and says, 'We won.'" Amid FedEx trucks and all sorts of delivery hubbub and shoppers in downtown Boston, Balmelli grabbed her in a big bear hug and they jumped up and down in joy.

Ed Balmelli and Michael Horgan

Dave Wilson and Rob Compton with Jake

Dave and Rob

Dave Wilson got the GLAD call at home after Rob Compton had left for work—his first day back on the job following the hip surgery that he'd put off for so long. Wilson picked him up and they returned home to learn the verdict from TV. Wilson remembers the media muddling through the implications of the court's decision to give the state 180 days before it began issuing marriage licenses to same-sex couples. But finally the reporters got it right: the SJC had issued a landmark ruling granting civil-marriage rights to same-sex couples. Wilson and their dog, Jake, jumped up and down in excitement, but not Compton—he was still on crutches. But he had calculated right. On the day of the big decision, he made it to the GLAD offices, to the press conference, and later to the GLAD community celebration at the Colonnade Hotel. He wouldn't miss this day.

The pre–press conference gathering at the GLAD offices pulsated with energy. As each plaintiff couple arrived, bursts of joyous laughter, hugs, tears, and amazed head-shaking filled the usually sedate and serious law offices. Coffee, juice, bagels, and fruit appeared. On one side of the room, Julie Goodridge sat and read a copy of the decision as Hillary, with a sweet smile of victory, looked on. Gary Chalmers and Gloria Bailey wept. Ellen Wade, grinning ear to ear, hugged Mary Bonauto.

THE VICTORY PRESS CONFERENCE

On the walk over to the Omni Parker House Hotel, Bonauto and the plaintiffs had TV, radio, and print media trailing them, jockeying for the best shots and sound bites. The proud smiles on the faces of the plaintiffs told it all. Bonauto began the press conference. "Wow, this is a very, very big day; it's obviously a historic day . . . because finally all families in the Commonwealth of Massachusetts will have the opportunity to be equal families under the law." With her voice ringing with conviction, Bonauto stated, "A court finally had the courage to say that this really is an issue about human equality and human dignity, and it's time that the government treat these people fairly."

Continuing her effort to ensure that Massachusetts did not adopt civil unions, Bonauto clearly asserted her understanding of the ruling: "The issue in this case was whether or not it was constitutional to exclude same-sex couples from civil, legal, and governmental marriages as well as all the protections that flow from that. That's what the court ruled on today. It didn't rule on a parallel system." Bonauto then insisted that the plaintiffs be allowed to speak.

Julie Goodridge pointed out that the court affirmed what they had always felt: "We are a couple that is worthy of the protections of marriage, and after sixteen and a half years Hillary and I are finally going to be able to get married and protect our family."

Gary Chalmers, with Rich Linnell at his side, told the assembled press, "My partner of fifteen years, finally after today, will be my official spouse come June. . . . We'll finally be able to have health insurance and so many other legal benefits we need to keep our family safe and secure."

Poignantly, Wilson and Smith, both African Americans, noted the important civil rights dimension of the decision. Wilson smiled as he asserted, "It means I'm a full citizen with all the rights of a citizen." Expanding on that point, Smith insisted, "The struggle for people to be treated equal is a long one, and it continues, and it gives me chills to think about that connection."

Facing page, top left
Julie Goodridge reads the decision as Hillary Goodridge looks on, clearly pleased.

Facing page, top right
Ed Balmelli runs into Mary Bonauto on the street outside the GLAD office.

Facing page, bottom
The plaintiffs, along with communications consultant Mary Breslauer (foreground, right) and attorney Mary Bonauto (backgroud, far right), walk from the GLAD offices to the Omni Parker House Hotel. Behind the Goodridges are plaintiffs Ellen Wade, Mike Horgan, and Linda Davies.

Toward the end of the press conference, the media questioned Bonauto again about why civil unions would not satisfy her clients. Her concise reply had probably been on her mind since the Vermont legislature invented civil unions: "We think the word *marriage* is one of the important protections because everybody knows what it means." A TV reporter then asked her if she would get married, and the usually very businesslike Bonauto looked down and then with a broad grin looked up and said, "You betcha!"

MARRIAGE OPPONENTS CRANK UP THE RHETORIC

Before the day ended, the justices of the SJC would be lionized as angels on the side of equality as well as branded as demonic forces of evil. At the State House, just two blocks from the victorious press conference, the opposition immediately began to muddy the waters, trying to create confusion about the meaning of the landmark decision. Governor Romney, a Mormon, declared that marriage should be between one man and one woman. Ignoring his own faith's history of polygamy, he asserted, "I agree with three thousand years of recorded history. I disagree with the Supreme Judicial Court of Massachusetts." He announced his support for an amendment to the Massachusetts constitution that would limit marriage to heterosexual couples.

Attorney General Thomas Reilly also challenged the legitimacy of the court's decision. "Such a profound change in social policy should have been decided by the legislature, not the courts," he declared. Days later, Arline Isaacson, cochair of the Massachusetts Gay and Lesbian Political Caucus, wryly tweaked him. "I kept thinking thank heavens he wasn't the attorney general when *Brown v. the Board of Education* was decided. Thank heavens he wasn't the attorney general when the anti-miscegenation laws were overturned. Because he would say, 'Oh no, the courts can't decide that; it should go to the Legislature.'"

Rumblings about the closeness of the 4–3 *Goodridge* decision were alluded to by the governor and other conservative critics. From London, nearly before the ink had dried on the SJC decision, President George W. Bush (a man who

Facing page
The clasped hands of plaintiff couple Gina Smith and Heidi Norton at the press conference.

became president by a 5–4 vote of the U.S. Supreme Court and who in July 2003 had responded to a question about same-sex marriage by beginning, "I am mindful that we're all sinners") shot another salvo: "Marriage is a sacred institution between a man and a woman. Today's decision of the Massachusetts Supreme Judicial Court violates this important principle."

Fueled by leading politicians' exploitation of the decision, conservative groups swung into action on Beacon Hill, across the state, and across the nation. At a State House press conference, Evelyn T. Reilly of the Massachusetts Family Institute called up specters of the AIDS epidemic: "Homosexual behavior . . . is extremely destructive to the human body, which was not designed for that activity." From the middle of the state, Laurie A. Letourneau of Shrewsbury, president of the Life Action League, ignored the bedrock principle of separation of church and state and declared, "This is truly a day of infamy brought on by a society who refuses to accept God and His teachings in their lives." As the leader of the Catholic Church in a predominantly Catholic state, Archbishop Sean O'Malley of the Boston Archdiocese began immediately to try to shape public opinion: "It is alarming that the Supreme Judicial Court in this ruling has cast aside . . . the very definition of marriage held by peoples for thousands of years."

EQUALITY ADVOCATES PRAISE THE DECISION

Not all Catholics, however, agreed with the church authorities. Senator Edward Kennedy greeted the *Goodridge* decision as "a welcome milestone on the road to full civil rights for all our citizens. Gay couples deserve these rights as well." Kennedy, as much as any politician, understood the importance of keeping the Church out of civil decision-making. Nearly forty-five years prior to the *Goodridge* decision, his brother John overcame the anti-Catholic prejudice of American voters by insisting that no church should "impose its will directly or indirectly upon the general populace or the public acts of its officials."

Many religious leaders celebrated the civil rights victory. The Reverend Nancy Taylor, president of the Massachusetts Conference of the United Church of Christ, exulted, "We have witnessed an extraordinary moment in Massachusetts history. . . . The court has affirmed that the quest for civil rights for all citizens will not be denied, either by prejudice or by religious doctrine." The Reverend William G. Sinkford, an African American and the president of the Unitarian Universalist Association, made an apt comparison with the *Brown* decision: "It affirms something which might not be popular at the time, but which is clearly morally right."

The renowned constitutional scholar and Harvard law professor Lawrence Tribe called the SJC decision "extremely gutsy." He laid bare the reality: "The Vermont decision basically says if you can identify some of the bells and whistles that come with marriage and call it something else, that's good enough. The SJC decision says, 'Let's stop kidding ourselves.'"

THE GAY AND LESBIAN COMMUNITY REJOICES

The *Goodridge* decision sent the gay and lesbian community into ecstasy. Seven hours after the GLAD press conference, an overflow crowd jammed into Boston's Old South Meeting House for a celebratory Rally for Family and Equality. In that very building in 1773, patriots had planned the Boston Tea Party. On November 18, 2003, the citizens of Massachusetts were there to kick off another revolution. Scott Gortikov and Ross Ozer sat in a church pew with their eighteen-month-old son, Sam, who waved an American flag. Gortikov said, "I actually feel proud to be an American today." Bridget Snell wrapped history and sports together: "There's a giddiness, like when the Patriots won the Super Bowl."

Across town at the Colonnade Hotel another overflow crowd jammed the main ballroom. GLAD's victorious attorney, Mary Bonauto, and her partner, Jennifer Wriggins, a University of Maine law professor; the plaintiff couples; and the MassEquality coalition partied on, despite knowing that their victory was not yet secure. The court's decision to put off the implementation of same-sex marriage for 180 days gave the opposition plenty of time to launch its campaign to overturn the ruling.

Preparing for the gathering storm, the Human Rights Campaign (HRC) pumped in more than $1 million for local and national advertising that heralded the victory and attempted to shore up support. A photo of the Goodridge family appeared in full-page ads in the *New York Times*, the *Boston Globe*, and other national newspapers on December 4 with the headline, "A Marriage License. Good for This Family. Good for *Every* Family." When conservatives threatened to block marriage licenses from being issued, Bonauto warned, "If marriage licenses aren't issued on Day 181, we will be back in court."

THE JOUSTING BEGINS

The population of Massachusetts is 50 percent Catholic, so it was no surprise that the Catholic Church became a lead player in opposing *Goodridge*. In early winter, most priests read letters at their Masses calling the SJC decision a "national tragedy." Marianne Duddy, a board member of Dignity, a gay Catholic group, looked at the Church reaction as desperate. "They think that they can pressure the legislature to overrule a direct court order. That's incredibly arrogant on the part of the Church officials."

Legislators who had failed for years to pass even limited protections for gay and lesbian families suddenly started looking at civil unions as a good compromise. On December 11, the state senate sent its civil-unions bill to the SJC for an advisory opinion. In an attempt to undo the *Goodridge* decision, the bill proposed the Vermont solution—same-sex couples would be granted the rights and benefits of marriage but without using the word *marriage*. Bonauto had carefully argued that the word *marriage* was in itself critical to marriage equality, because everyone—from hospital staff to insurance salesmen—knew what it meant. But would the justices give in on this one point? Openly gay state senator Jarrett Barrios bemoaned the shenanigans of his col-

A marriage license:

Hillary, Annie and Julie Goodridge

© Marilyn Humphries

Good for this family. Good for *every* family.

Something remarkable just happened for Massachusetts families like Hillary and Julie Goodridge and their daughter, Annie.

The highest court in Massachusetts said it was wrong for the government to deny marriage licenses – and the important protections they provide – to committed gay and lesbian couples and their families.

For families like the Goodridges, the decision was monumental.

But it was also simple. It didn't make any person change his or her religious beliefs. And it didn't tell any church or other religious institution what relationships it has to recognize.

All it did was recognize that equality and fairness are core principles under the Constitution; and that love, commitment and responsibility are important values in any relationship.

Access to marriage does more than provide families with important protections – such as visiting one another in the hospital, and getting full Social Security benefits and inheritance rights if a partner dies.

When Americans like the Goodridges have access to marriage, it makes their family stronger and more stable. And it makes society stronger and more stable as well.

Unfortunately, hard-working, tax-paying families – who, like the Goodridges, take on all the responsibilities of a long-term committed relationship – are still denied these critical protections in every other state in America.

Legal protection for Hillary, Julie and Annie is one small step toward making America stronger and fairer. But it's time we honored love, commitment and family for all Americans.

HUMAN RIGHTS CAMPAIGN
FOUNDATION

All families deserve protection.

For more information: www.hrc.org.

HRC salutes Gay & Lesbian Advocates & Defenders (www.GLAD.org) for their work on behalf of the Goodridges and devoted couples in Massachusetts.

Paid for by the Human Rights Campaign Foundation

leagues: "I continue to be disappointed by the legislative back-flips which Governor Romney and some legislators are performing in the effort to discriminate against gay and lesbian people in the wake of this court decision."

BACK FROM THE HOLIDAYS

The holiday season anesthetized the public posturing for a while. The calm broke on January 5, 2004, when three former high-ranking Massachusetts officials—attorneys general Scott Harshbarger and James Shannon and former governor William Weld—along with Renee Landers, president of the Boston Bar Association, and constitutional scholar Laurence Tribe sent a letter to all legislators asking them to uphold the decision of the SJC in favor of same-sex marriage. "There is no legal justification for creating a new and separate legal status for gay people given the Court's ruling that the exclusion from marriage is itself unconstitutional." The letter carefully argued that the *Goodridge* decision could not be interpreted as supporting civil unions as an alternative to marriage. The holiday truce was over.

On January 7, the conservatives shot back. Ron Crews of the Massachusetts Family Institute (MFI) and state representative Philip Travis held a press conference and rally at the State House to announce their new Coalition for Marriage, made up of the Catholic Church, Focus on the Family, the Black Ministerial Alliance, the Family Research Council, Concerned Women for America, and the Alliance Defense Fund. They voiced their support for amendments to the constitution to define marriage as a union between one man and one woman and a further amendment that called for the election of judges every six years. Despite the fact that the coalition had thrown a wide net to gain support, only a hundred people turned out for their event.

On the following day, more than a thousand people rallied with MassEquality, a broad coalition of gay and lesbian, civil rights, labor, professional, religious, and community groups, at the State House. Mass Gay and Lesbian Political Caucus cochair Gary Daffin, an African American Catholic from Alabama, responded to some of the hate that had emanated from the previous day's rally. "I come from Alabama, and so we're very acquainted with the language of segregation, and when I was listening yesterday . . . I could hear the echo of George Wallace . . . 'Segregation today, segregation tomorrow, segregation forever.' And so we're here today to say something very, very simple which is this: Separate but equal does not work."

AWAITING THE COURT'S ADVISORY OPINION

The national attacks on same-sex marriage continued. In his State of the Union address on January 20, 2004, President Bush went out of his way to discuss the sanctity of marriage. In the gallery, San Francisco mayor Gavin Newsom heard the president's words on marriage, and their simple injustice inspired him to act. On his return to San Francisco, Newsom set in motion his decision to begin issuing marriage licenses to same-sex couples in San Francisco, an act that would inspire other mayors similarly to defy the law in their localities throughout the winter and spring of 2004.

The Coalition for Marriage ran a full-page ad in the *Boston Globe* on January 23 that claimed gay parents were "an unproven social experiment." The group managed to offend all adoptive parents by pointing to a study (supported by no reputable scholars or clinicians) that asserted that children living in homes with one or more non-biological parents are eight times more likely to die of maltreatment.

By now it was bitterly cold in Massachusetts, and both sides plotted their strategies for the upcoming constitutional convention. Neither group considered outdoor rallies—not in that weather. But when the Massachusetts Voices for Traditional Marriage (VTM) held three rallies on January 25 in gyms at Catholic schools across the state, outside each of the schools, in single-digit temperatures, supporters of same-sex marriage stood holding signs and bearing witness to the dignity of their lives and their aspirations for civil marriage. Laurie Letourneau of VTM declared, "It's about judicial tyranny. We have the right to vote. . . ." Arline Isaacson of Mass Gay and Lesbian Political Caucus articulated what many in the gay and lesbian community were feeling as win-

Top
Ron Crews, president of the
Massachusetts Family Institute,
announcing the Coalition
for Marriage.

Bottom
Bishop Gilbert Thompson
of Boston's Black Ministerial
Alliance speaks at the anti-gay
Coalition for Marriage rally at
the Massachusetts State House.

ter settled in: "They are dressing up their bigotry with arguments about democracy, and they pretend that the courts should not have made this decision, but they would not have objected to the court making the decision if the court had decided their way. . . . It is fundamentally un-American for the tyranny of the majority to determine the rights of any minority."

GOODRIDGE AND MARRIAGE REAFFIRMED

On February 4, 2004, the court issued an advisory opinion on the state senate's civil-unions bill, which had been offered as an alternative to gay marriage. The visitor gallery was packed as the opinion was read into the record. The court issued a point-by-point rejection of civil unions. Eloquently highlighting the civil rights dimension of *Goodridge*, the justices wrote, "The history of our nation has demonstrated that separate is seldom, if ever, equal." They then answered the question on legislators' minds: "Are civil unions good enough?" With blunt concluding words, the court declared, "The answer to the question is 'No.'" At that resounding "No," the gallery exploded into cheers and applause.

Overjoyed with the decision, GLAD once again held a victory press conference at the Omni Parker House Hotel. Bonauto began, "Today any confusion that anyone may have had in his or her own mind about what the court meant in its historic ruling on November 18, 2003, has now been laid to rest." She emphasized, "For those folks who support equality now, it's clear that the thing to do is stand by the *Goodridge* decision and to oppose any effort to write discrimination into our constitution in Massachusetts."

THE PERFECT STORM GATHERS

So in a state made famous for a perfect storm, another storm—energized by clashing political, religious, and cultural forces—gathered momentum one week before the state constitutional convention. Predictably, Governor Romney denounced the court's advisory opinion. "We've heard from the court, but not from the people. The people of Massachusetts should not be excluded

from a decision as fundamental to our society as the definition of marriage."
C. J. Doyle of the Catholic Action League encouraged legislators to impeach
the four "offending" justices who ruled as the majority. But Gary Chalmers,
a plaintiff from the middle of the state, remained thrilled: "I think and hope
this will help push people along to convince them that this is our constitutional right." And from the farthest reaches of the state, plaintiff Gina Smith
continued on the theme of civil rights: "I'm glad the court said again that the
constitution requires that we be treated equally. . . . I'm happy that I can plan
on marrying the person who loves me."

GLAD attorney Mary Bonauto (front, right) and plaintiffs (L-R) Ellen Wade, Julie Goodridge, Ed Balmelli (back), Hillary Goodridge, Dave Wilson, and Rob Compton are jubilant as they prepare for the press conference at the Omni Parker House Hotel.

I am hopeful that our decision will be accepted by those thoughtful citizens who believe that same-sex unions should not be approved by the state. I am not referring here to acceptance in the sense of grudging acknowledgment of the court's authority to adjudicate the matter. My hope is more liberating. The plaintiffs are members of our community, our neighbors, our coworkers, our friends. As pointed out by the court, their professions include investment advisor, computer engineer, therapist, and lawyer. The plaintiffs volunteer in our schools, worship beside us in our religious houses, and have children who play with our children, to mention just a few ordinary daily contacts. We share a common humanity and participate together in the social contract that is the foundation of our commonwealth. Simple principles of decency dictate that we extend to the plaintiffs, and to their new status, full acceptance, tolerance, and respect. We should do so because it is the right thing to do.

—*Justice John Greaney, concurring opinion in* Goodridge v. Department of Public Health

Gay and lesbian demonstrators on December 7, 1987, picketing outside the State House to demand that the senate vote on the lesbian and gay civil rights bill.

CHAPTER 2

EARLY MILESTONES

The Struggle for Family Equality

It is no surprise that our community had to go to the courts and say, "Please address our grievances, our concerns," because the legislature has reneged on its responsibilities. . . . We didn't get to this day by chance. . . . [And] we are not going away. We will be here fighting until we are recognized as fully equal under the law.

—*Representative Carl M. Sciortino*

In June 1972, Boston's newly emerging gay and lesbian community came out for their third gay pride celebration, marching down Boylston Street to the Boston Common in their annual commemoration of the day gay men and lesbians fought back—June 28, 1969. It was on that day that patrons of a New York gay bar, the Stonewall Inn, had resisted a routine police raid and galvanized a new era of gay activism nationwide.

The 1972 gay pride march included a new face—a candidate for Boston's Beacon Hill seat in the state legislature, Barney Frank. Closeted and fearful of revealing his own sexuality, Frank nonetheless determined that he could both help—and be helped by—this new emerging force in state politics. He pledged to introduce a gay rights bill in the state legislature if he was elected.

Frank went on to win the Beacon Hill seat, and he immediately introduced a bill to ban discrimination against gay men and lesbians in housing, employment, insurance, credit, and public accommodations. It was a significant step in the gay community's emerging civil rights struggle. Nonetheless, it took seventeen years before the legislation passed—many years after Barney Frank became a U.S. congressman and, eventually, an openly gay public official. It was a full three decades of struggle on many fronts before the gay and lesbian community celebrated marriage equality in 2003.

Massachusetts, in many respects, has been ahead of much of the country in ending discrimination against gay men and lesbians. Though predominantly Catholic, the state has deep traditions of fairness and equality, codified in its 225-year-old constitution, that have provided fertile ground on which to build a gay rights movement. With its many colleges and universities, Boston not surprisingly emerged as a center of the gay liberation movement in the early seventies. One of the movement's most progressive voices—*Gay Community News*—began publishing in 1973; it served as a catalyst for the gay rights struggle locally and nationally. In 1974, Bostonians elected Elaine Noble to the state's house of representatives; she was the first openly gay state legislator in the nation.

Facing page
On November 18, 1989, former Massachusetts state representative Elaine Noble was honored at the people's signing of the gay rights bill at Faneuil Hall.

As in major cities across the country, the early years of gay liberation in Massachusetts were about coming out—making gay men and lesbians a visible part of the community—and securing basic civil rights. For decades, lesbians and gay men had hidden their sexual orientation for fear of losing jobs or housing or being the target of hate crimes. In the post-Stonewall era, pride inspired a new openness. Lesbians, especially in Cambridge, Boston, and Northampton, created rich cultural environments, including women's bookstores, magazines and newspapers, restaurants, bars, music, and co-ops. Much of their political activity, however, was focused on feminist causes such as passing the Massachusetts Equal Rights Amendment; exposing and responding to domestic violence, rape, and incest; protecting reproductive freedom; and achieving equality for women in the workforce. Gay men turned neighborhoods such as Boston's South End and the beach community of Provincetown into enclaves where gay culture, including theater, arts, restaurants and bars, flourished. New gay political organizations sought to overturn Massachusett's colonial sodomy statutes and end police harassment.

Two organizations emerged in the 1970s that would become critical to the struggle for equality. The Massachusetts Gay and Lesbian Political Caucus (MGLPC), founded in 1973, became the State House lobby for the gay community, slowly building a legislative majority for the gay civil rights measure. Gay & Lesbian Advocates & Defenders (GLAD), founded in 1978, fought for the same rights through the courts. In addition, multiple grassroots organizations—from the Daughters of Bilitis, the Homophile Union of Boston, and the Gay Liberation Front in the 1970s to the Gay and Lesbian Political Alliance, ACT UP, Queer Nation, and Lesbian Avengers in later years—used demonstrations, media, lobbying, and community organizing to increase visibility and challenge stereotypes of gay men and lesbians as isolated, sick, and sinful people, undeserving of equal rights.

WHY MARRIAGE?

By the late 1970s, Massachusetts gay men and lesbians had made significant strides toward respect and acceptance. Though the gay rights bill, reintroduced in each legislative session, remained stalled, changes were happening in the community. Among lesbians, there was increasing talk of motherhood. In January 1979, the Lesbian and Gay Parents Project opened in Cambridge to provide resources and assistance to parents denied custody because of their sexual orientation and to educate the public about gay and lesbian families. The group hoped to counter stereotypes of gay men and lesbians as threatening to children and as marginal people living outside the boundaries of the "normal" family.

As lesbian mothers came out and fought for custody of their children, they inspired a new trend—lesbians having children on their own. By the mid-1980s, the lesbian baby boom was dramatically changing lesbian communities locally and nationally.

In 1984, stirred by new conversations concerning motherhood and family, local filmmaker Deborah Chasnoff produced the film *Choosing Children*. A 1988 conference on parenting, Children in Our Lives, attracted more than eight hundred women from around New England, and discussion groups for lesbians exploring motherhood were regularly advertised in the local gay and feminist newspapers. As lesbians pushing strollers became a common sight at gay pride marches, legal issues became more salient. How could same-sex parents—who had no legal relationship to each other—ensure that they had legally recognized relationships to their children? Not only were wills, trusts, powers of attorney, and medical proxies costly, they weren't adequate to protect family relationships. For many, the right to marry was becoming more urgent. Only marriage offered families real security.

In the 1980s, gay men confronted a different set of family challenges brought on by the AIDS epidemic. As thousands of gay men succumbed to illness and death, their partners, devastated by loss, faced exhausting legal challenges. Their rights to hospital visitation and medical decisions could be

By June 1988, lesbian moms with baby strollers were a common sight at Boston's annual Pride Parade.

overturned by parents who may not have seen their sons for years. At death, homes and possessions could be lost to distant family members or to landlords who refused to recognize a "roommate" who hadn't signed the lease. A gay man couldn't access family health benefits for his sick partner forced to leave his job, nor could he receive pension or Social Security benefits after his partner's death. For gay men, as well as for sympathetic heterosexual family members, friends, and health care providers, AIDS brought into sharp relief the fragility of relationships that lacked any form of legal recognition.

A new militant activism swept gay and lesbian communities in response to AIDS. Angry at the government's neglect of the crisis, gay men and lesbians burst through the closet doors and demanded respect for their communities. Boston's annual gay pride marches in the 1980s swelled to tens of thousands, including large contingents of straight supporters in groups such as Parents and Friends of Lesbians and Gays (PFLAG), the American Civil Liberties Union (ACLU) of Massachusetts, and progressive religious congregations such as the Unitarian Universalists.

In preparation for a national gay rights march on Washington, the gay community developed an advertising campaign; on subway cars, they placed placards reading COME OUT FOR YOURSELVES. COME OUT FOR YOUR FRIENDS. COME OUT FOR JUSTICE. In that spirit more than a half-million gay men and lesbians gathered in Washington, D.C., on October 11, 1987, to remind the nation that "Silence = Death." In a visceral expression of communal grief and rage sparked by the AIDS crisis, hundreds of thousands gathered for a candlelight vigil at the Washington Monument reflecting pool. The nation was put on notice: The gay community would not go quiet into the night.

This page
In the spring of 1988, ACT UP/Boston brought its protest against discriminatory treatment of people with AIDS in housing, insurance, and medical care to Quincy Market, one of the centers of tourism in the city. Raymond Schmidt and Stephen Skuce hold the signature ACT UP banner.

Facing page
AIDS candlelight vigil, October 11, 1987, Washington Monument reflecting pool.

On November 15, 1989, Governor Dukakis signed the gay rights bill
into law. Massachusetts became the second state, after Wisconsin, to pass such a bill. As two hundred activists and supporters
cheered, MGLPC cochair Arline Isaacson acknowledged the crowd
by signing I love you. Standing are some of the bill's key supporters
(L-R): Rep. Marjorie Clapprood; Rep. Barbara Hildt; Rep. Mark Roosevelt; cochair of MGLPC Steven Tierney; Isaacson; Sen. Mike Bar-
rett; Gov. Michael Dukakis; Atty. Gen. Jim Shannon; Rep. Lois
Pines; Sen. William Golden; and Rep. Joseph Mackey.

FOSTER EQUALITY

The AIDS crisis ratcheted up homophobic fear and hatred. In fact, national polls showed that in the mid-eighties, anti-gay sentiment reached an all-time high. It was in this context of increasing gay visibility and homophobic backlash that Donald Babets and David Jean, two professional, churchgoing gay men who lived in Boston, decided that they wanted to bring children into their lives. Hearing that there was a shortage of foster parents and finding no rules that barred gay men from applying, they began the process of filling out questionnaires, undergoing an extensive home study, and attending the requisite training. After almost a year's time and special review by the associate commissioner of the Department of Social Services (DSS), they were approved as foster parents.

In April 1985, DSS called Babets and Jean and asked them to take two brothers, Richard, three, and John, twenty-two months. The fathers-to-be bought diapers, clothes, and toys and began the process of making a family. They gave the boys love and stability, and by early May the new fathers and the children were beginning to feel a sense of comfort and trust. Then on May 8, the *Boston Globe* Metro section led with the headline, "Some Oppose Foster Placement with Gay Couple." The sensationalist story relied heavily on quotes from neighbors who disapproved of the state's decision to allow Babets and Jean to become foster parents.

DSS called that morning to assure Babets and Jean that the children would not be taken away, but at two that afternoon, social workers arrived to take Richard and John to another home. It appeared that the governor's office had overruled the DSS social workers. In a statement to the press, Babets and Jean said, "We wish to make it clear that we believe that the removal of the boys from our home was not in their best interest. To see them leave us—angry, confused and in tears—was one of the most difficult moments of our lives."

The next day, Governor Michael Dukakis ordered a review of the state's foster-care policies, which resulted in a hierarchy of placement that essentially

The administration is exploiting people's worst fears and stereotypes that gay people are child molesters for its own political self-interest.

—Cathy Hoffman, spokesperson
for the Gay and Lesbian Defense
Committee, May 1985

excluded gay men and lesbians from providing homes for abused and neglected children. Enraged by the state's cavalier attitude toward Babets and Jean's family and by the underlying premise of the new foster-care guidelines—that gay men and lesbians are inferior parents and, by implication, people—the community fought back. Almost immediately, activists formed the Gay and Lesbian Defense Committee. Their focus—overturning a policy based on ignorance and prejudice and ending discrimination against gay and lesbian families—propelled Massachusetts toward a new relationship with its gay and lesbian citizens.

The Foster Equality campaign incited the state's first public debate on gay and lesbian families. Professional associations of social workers, psychologists, and psychiatrists all spoke out against the state policy, arguing that no evidence suggested that children raised by same-sex parents were any less healthy or well adjusted than those raised by heterosexuals. Nonetheless, the *Boston Globe* editorialized, "The goal of foster care is to remove a child from an *abnormal* home setting and place him in as *normal* a home setting as possible. For foster children, the most *normal* home setting—even if it is no longer statistically the most prevalent—is clearly that of a married man and woman with two or three children of their own [emphasis added]."

The outraged gay community organized multiple boisterous street demonstrations. On Father's Day, gay and lesbian protesters marched through the streets of Brookline to the governor's home, where they served him with a 51-A, a child-abuse complaint. Foster Equality stickers and flyers asking ARE YOU A NORMAL FAMILY? appeared all over the state. A sit-in at the State House forced Governor Dukakis to meet with Babets and Jean, along with other gay and lesbian parents and supporters, but Dukakis remained firmly committed to placing children in "traditional families."

For five years, the foster-care policy remained a highly contentious issue. The legislature demonstrated its own bias against gay and lesbian parenting by several times proposing budget riders that claimed "a homosexual or bisexual orientation shall be considered an obstacle to the psychological well-

Facing page, top right
On Father's Day, June 16, 1985, about five hundred gay men, lesbians, and supporters marched to Governor Michael Dukakis's home, carrying the banner NORMAL? NEVER! in response to a *Boston Globe* editorial that suggested that foster children should be placed in "normal" homes. Holding the banner are Ann Holder and Margaret Cerullo and on the far left are Marla Erlien and Cathy Hoffman, all leaders in the Gay and Lesbian Defense Committee.

Facing page, bottom left
The high-profile Foster Equality campaign haunted Governor Dukakis for years. These signs, placed on the State House fence, urged the community to boycott the Duke (Dukakis) in the November 4, 1986, gubernatorial election.

Facing page, bottom right
On October 13, 1993, members of the Governor's Commission on Gay and Lesbian Youth and hundreds of student supporters gathered at the State House to lobby for passage of the gay and lesbian student rights bill. Two months later, Governor William Weld signed the bill into law.

being of a child." Not even the governor would sign a measure so clearly opposed by the vast majority of the state's child development specialists.

Finally, in 1990, a lawsuit filed by the American Civil Liberties Union and GLAD on behalf of Babets and Jean resolved the issue with an out-of-court settlement in which the state agreed to rescind the regulations and return to the standard of "the best interests of the child." In response to the settlement, one lesbian mother said, "I am thrilled. What the [old] policy said to me was that as lesbians and gay men, you're not okay to be with children. And that's saying you're not okay, period. It's a much broader kind of annihilation."

The foster-care controversy and the AIDS crisis exposed people's fears of homosexuality, forcing the gay and lesbian community to regroup and build stronger allies among those who believed that all citizens of the commonwealth deserved equality. In the late eighties, through the work of the gay community in educating lawmakers and the public, compassion replaced fear, and a less hostile environment emerged. As a result, in 1989 the state legislature finally passed the gay and lesbian civil rights bill, and Governor Dukakis, still considered no friend of the gay community, signed it into law.

GAY YOUTH COME OUT

For the Massachusetts gay and lesbian community, the political stars aligned in the early 1990s. Attorney General James Shannon refused to certify a conservative Citizens for Families First referendum question intended to overturn the 1989 gay rights law. The new governor, Republican William Weld, appointed openly gay officials and by executive order established a domestic-partners registry for state workers as well as the Gay and Lesbian Youth Commission.

As a result of the work of the Youth Commission, Massachusetts passed a pioneering gay and lesbian student rights law in 1993 and instituted a Safe Schools program that continues to support gay youth today. Beginning in 1995, gay–straight alliances at public schools and youth pride marches made

This is a civil rights bill. It simply says that rights most of us take for granted should not be denied to others. In Massachusetts today gay men and lesbians can be and are fired, denied housing and credit, and they have no legal recourse.

—*Representative Mark Roosevelt, May 1987*

young gay people visible to the community at large. Earnest, vulnerable, and passionate about their identities, these young people challenged the common misunderstanding that gay men and lesbians choose their lifestyle. Speaking out for themselves and their futures, gay youth became a visible counterweight to increasingly hostile social and religious conservatives who were attempting to use homophobia to reshape Massachusetts's liberal political culture.

LEGALIZING FAMILY RELATIONS

The 1989 civil rights law barred discrimination against gay individuals but did nothing to protect their families. In the early nineties, the courts and the legislature still had little understanding of the challenges facing gay and lesbian partners and their children. One thing had changed, however: in the wake of the Foster Equality campaign, the AIDS crisis, and the seventeen-year struggle to pass the civil rights law, gay men and lesbians were now living their lives openly in communities across the commonwealth. More and more people—including lawmakers—personally knew colleagues, neighbors, friends, or family members who were openly gay.

With a more supportive administration on Beacon Hill and a nondiscrimination law protecting basic civil rights, the gay and lesbian community turned to the issue of family rights. In 1991, the gay employees of Cambridge-based Lotus Development Corporation were among the first in the country to win domestic-partnership benefits from a private company. The MGLPC, hoping to win similar benefits for Massachusetts public employees, pushed legislative allies to introduce a domestic-partnership bill in 1993.

Feeling that the legislature was still uncomfortable with gay relationships, Arline Isaacson of MGLPC argued that the best way to win domestic partnership was to frame the issue in terms of equal benefits. In a hearing on the bill, Isaacson made her case by asking legislators to imagine two employees working side by side. "The one who just got hired is able to have his wife's [insurance] covered by the company, but the one who has been there for twenty-five years can't have his partner covered. That's discrimination," she insisted.

Despite Isaacson's persistent efforts, the domestic-partnership bill languished in the house of representatives, where the leadership, influenced by the Catholic Church, remained firmly against recognition of gay families. Communities around the state, however, were moving more quickly. In the early 1990s, Boston, Brewster, Brookline, and Cambridge all passed dometic-partnership ordinances. Although these ordinances affected a small number of city employees only, they served to further legitimize same-sex partnerships.

With domestic partnership stalled in the State House, gay and lesbian attorneys turned to the courts to build a legal foundation for gay and lesbian family rights. In 1993, the Massachusetts Supreme Judicial Court (SJC) ruled that the nonbiological parent in a same-sex couple could adopt his or her partner's child; this allowed a child to have two parents of the same sex. The ruling also opened the way for same-sex couples to adopt children together.

The second-parent adoption case established a clear precedent recognizing gay and lesbian families. Although same-sex partners still had no legal relationship to each other, nonbiological parents could now firmly assert their parental rights. But most important, as plaintiff Ellen Wade noted, the court ruling meant that when she and her partner, Maureen Brodoff, returned to the lower court for adoption proceedings, they and their daughter, Kate, "would be recognized as what they are—a family."

Family recognition was also on the minds of lesbians and gay men when they returned to Washington, D.C., in April 1993 for another national demonstration. Thousands of same-sex couples gathered in front of the IRS building to participate in a mass wedding and to draw attention to the thousand-plus federal benefits, many of them tax-related, that are denied same-sex partners excluded from civil marriage.

Increasingly, lesbians and gay men felt that without marriage equality, not only would they continue to suffer legal and financial hardships, but no matter how long they were together, their relationships would never be accorded the same respect as those of married heterosexuals.

*T*he first line of protection is coming out. You must come out! We spent nine years and $225,000 to arrive at a 1991 appellate court decision . . . that called us a "family of affinity."

—Karen Thompson, April 1993, speaking at the Marriage Ceremony at the 1993 March on Washington

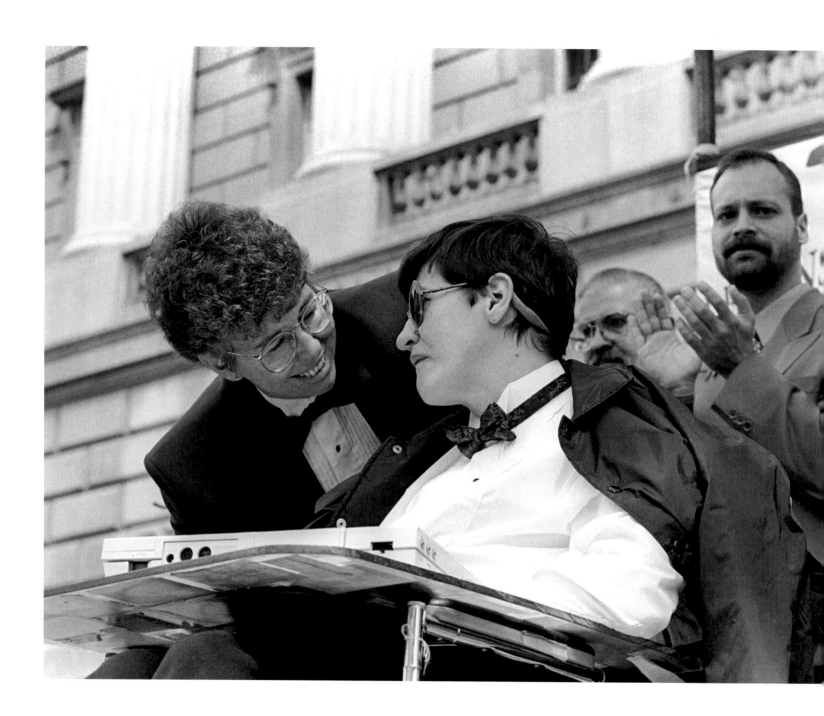

$\mathcal{W}$e thought it would be a good idea to wear these gowns to give the parade route viewers an image of two women in gowns. We especially wanted the kids to have this image (one we never had growing up). The reception was overwhelming.

—Jackie Fein-Zachary

Facing page
At Boston's annual lesbian and gay pride parade in 1999, Valerie and Jackie Fein-Zachary wore the gowns from their 1995 wedding.

At a 1996 rally in support of domestic partnership, two protesters suggested they were not willing to settle for anything less than full relationship recognition—that is, marriage.

DOMA DEFEAT OPENS DOOR FOR MARRIAGE EQUALITY

Since the early 1970s, when gay men and lesbians first began demanding the right to be who they are without facing discrimination, social and religious conservatives have tried desperately to slam the closet door shut. So, too, in Massachusetts, gay men and lesbians have had to resist constant attempts to undermine gains made in the legislature and the courts. In the 1990s, these attacks, led by Christian fundamentalists and the Catholic Church, became increasingly coordinated and effective.

In the mid-1990s, religious conservatives, sometimes using stealth tactics to hide their anti-sex education, pro-abstinence, anti-gay agenda, attempted to take over local school boards in Newton and Braintree, among other communities. Lawsuits brought by the right-wing American Center for Law and Justice on behalf of the Catholic Action League in 1999 and 2000 challenged domestic-partnership laws in Boston and Cambridge. These lawsuits effectively overturned efforts by municipalities throughout the state to offer equal benefits to same-sex couples. Beginning in 1998, a series of Defense of Marriage Acts (DOMA), modeled on the 1996 federal law defining marriage as the "union of one man and one woman," were introduced in the Massachusetts legislature. When these bills did not succeed, Massachusetts Citizens for Marriage announced, in July 2001, a petition drive to put the gay marriage question on the ballot in 2004.

A coalition of gay and civil liberties organizations—including the Freedom to Marry Coalition, MGLPC, GLAD, the Religious Coalition for the Freedom to Marry, and the ACLU of Massachusetts, among others—quickly formed MassEquality to defeat the ballot petition. In a dress rehearsal for the post-*Goodridge* amendment battles, Massachusetts plunged into a nasty, expensive street fight over the local DOMA threat to equal marriage. The *Boston Globe* called the petition drive and the effort to defeat it "the fiercest battle over gay rights in Massachusetts in more than a decade," and noted that "it is being fought face-to-face at neighborhood supermarkets, shopping malls, and T stops, often in a less than civil manner."

*W*e have been expecting the Christian Coalition to target us for some time. The city is going to come out fighting.

—*Representative Jarrett Barrios, March 22, 2000*

As required, once the ballot petitions were certified by state attorney general Tom Reilly, senate president Tom Birmingham convened a constitutional convention—a joint session of the legislature—to consider the proposed DOMA. Pressed by gay and lesbian activists to allow more time for constituents to talk with their representatives, Birmingham opened the 2002 convention in June but then immediately called for a recess until July. As he gaveled the session to a close, the senate president was stunned by an outburst from the chamber's gallery, where amendment proponents had gathered. Birmingham recalled "a thundercloud of boos coming from the gallery. . . . It was the voice of hatred. . . . From that moment on, nothing surprised me."

When the convention reconvened, on July 17, 2002, Birmingham had made a decision. Bombarded by hate mail during the preceding month and believing the amendment was "wrong-hearted, mean-spirited, discriminatory and unfair," he used his position as senate leader to help defeat the measure. Under the rules of the legislature, only one quarter of the members (fifty) would need to vote yes on the amendment to move it forward to the next constitutional convention and then to the ballot in 2004. Rather than allowing a small minority to keep the measure alive, Birmingham immediately called for a vote on a motion to adjourn. That vote provided an opportunity for legislators, the majority of whom opposed the amendment, to defeat it.

In an interview in *Bay Windows* several months later, he explained, "Everyone voting on it knew what the significance of the adjournment vote was. I thought that was the proper balance of forwarding the drive to set back [the anti-gay amendment] and also respecting the democratic process. We had a roll call vote, and I was very proud of the members when we overwhelmingly [137–53] voted to adjourn."

The target of right-wing vitriol and hate, including death threats, Birmingham lost his bid for the Democratic gubernatorial nomination. For gay men and lesbians and their allies, however, he was a rare hero—a man who acted on his convictions despite the political price. He saved Massa-

Facing page
On March 22, 2000, Jarrett Barrios, Cambridge's openly gay state representative, confronted William Monahan, counsel for the Catholic Action League of Massachusetts, outside Cambridge City Hall. The league had recently filed a lawsuit challenging the city's domestic-partner ordinance.

When senate president Tom Birmingham allowed
the 2002 constitutional convention to adjourn
without voting on the DOMA, Laurie Letourneau
(center), a leader of the conservative Massachusetts Citizens for Marriage, angrily protested
outside the chamber.

chusetts from writing discrimination into its constitution by expressly prohibiting marriage for same-sex couples.

A MARRIAGE REVOLUTION

Religious and social conservatives continued to press for a DOMA amendment in Massachusetts, but the facts on the ground were changing too quickly for their efforts to gain traction. Mary Bonauto had filed *Goodridge* in 2001, in part because she knew the anti-gay marriage ballot initiative was on the horizon. Her assumption that the lawsuit would serve as an important public education tool, mobilizing gay men and lesbians as well as allies in the fight for same-sex marriage, proved correct. The *Goodridge* plaintiffs became ambassadors for gay and lesbian families across the state, putting real faces on what for some was a frightening concept. With the plaintiffs in the public eye, the MassEquality coalition grew to include a vast array of civil liberties, religious, and economic justice organizations that had not previously fought for gay and lesbian civil rights.

Following the defeat of the DOMA amendment, a new confidence drove the same-sex marriage movement. Though Mitt Romney, who said things like "Call me old-fashioned, but I don't support gay marriage nor do I support civil unions," won the November 2002 gubernatorial election, energy among marriage equality activists remained high. In March 2003, the SJC heard oral arguments in the *Goodridge* case. In October, marriage equality supporters in the legislature filed two civil-union bills and a same-sex marriage bill. Public events, coupled with an advertising campaign by the Human Rights Campaign featuring the Massachusetts same-sex couples, kept the marriage issue alive in the press. With polls showing marriage equality gaining favor, Archbishop Sean O'Malley took time away from rehabilitating the Church's image in the wake of the clergy child sexual abuse scandal to pronounce gay marriage "an attack on the common good." It seemed that on both sides of the issue preparations were under way for a major confrontation.

Finally, on November 18, 2003, the supreme judicial court issued its decision. Writing for the majority, Chief Justice Margaret Marshall confirmed that for same-sex couples, full equality includes the right to civil marriage:

> Limiting the protections, benefits, and obligations of civil marriage to opposite-sex couples violates the basic premises of individual liberty and equality under law protected by the Massachusetts Constitution.

Pausing to absorb this astonishing confirmation of their citizenship rights, gay men and lesbians and their supporters celebrated a joyous holiday season. Then they prepared for the onslaught—a new phase in the struggle for marriage equality was about to begin.

There are some issues where I feel strongly that you do not wet your finger and hold it to the wind. There are some issues where you just do what is right. . . . This issue is one of those core issues; it is not a function of polling or what advances you that decides your stance.

—*Senator Tom Birmingham, December 2002*

At the February 15, 2003, Massachusetts Freedom to Marry Coalition fund-raiser, FTMC cochair Valerie Fein-Zachary, FTMC advocacy director Josh Friedes, and state senator Cheryl Jacques honored former state senate president Tom Birmingham with the Freedom to Marry Hero Award.

Thousands of citizens descended on the State
House during the constitutional convention.

CHAPTER 3

SEPARATE BUT EQUAL?

Defending Marriage Equality

The history of our nation has demonstrated that separate is seldom, if ever, equal.

—*Massachusetts Supreme Judicial Court*

A constitutional amendment banning same-sex marriages is a form of gay-bashing and it would do nothing at all to protect traditional marriages.

—*Coretta Scott King*

"The answer to the question is 'No.'" With these blunt concluding words in its February 4, 2004, advisory opinion, the Massachusetts Supreme Judicial Court (SJC) made clear to legislators that they could not, as they had hoped, circumvent the *Goodridge* decision with a civil-unions bill. Marriage, and only marriage, for same-sex couples would pass constitutional muster. For the legislature, that left only one avenue for overturning the court decision: a constitutional amendment defining *marriage* as exclusively heterosexual—a so-called Defense of Marriage Act (DOMA). Massachusetts had held firm in defeating similar DOMAs in previous legislative sessions, but with gay marriage looming, the political stakes had changed. Post *Goodridge*, it was a whole new ball game. Voters would be watching, and elections were imminent.

Massachusetts was about to embark on a huge civics lesson. The bedrock American value of equality tested in the court with *Goodridge* would be put to the test in the legislature. The multiyear process for amending the Massachusetts constitution meant that even if the legislators passed an amendment in the 2004 constitutional convention, they could not stop same-sex weddings, which the court had ordered to begin on May 17. Any amendment would have to be voted on again by the legislature in 2005 and approved by the voters in a 2006 ballot referendum. Given the chance, would voters two years hence annul the marriages of thousands of gay and lesbian couples? That remained to be seen. The only thing the gay and lesbian community could count on was that their families, so long invisible, would dominate the public conversation for months—and possibly years—to come.

CITIZENS MARSHAL THEIR FORCES

With the legislature now in the driver's seat, attention turned to influencing votes on Beacon Hill. Citizens on both sides of the issue marshaled their forces. On February 8, the newly formed Coalition for Marriage, an alliance of the Catholic Church and conservative family values organizations such as Focus on the Family, the Family Research Council, and Concerned Women

or those legislators who think civil unions are acceptable, I would ask, "Would they substitute their marriage for a civil union certificate?"

—Goodridge *plaintiff Gina Smith*

Facing page
MassEquality held numerous candlelight vigils in support of same-sex marriage.

Religious fundamentalists believed that their
biblical message would sway legislators to vote
against marriage equality.

for America, drew two thousand marriage equality opponents to Boston Common. Chanting "Let the people vote," they demanded that legislators pass a DOMA amendment to the Massachusetts constitution.

MassEquality, the coalition fighting for marriage equality, feared the economic firepower of the Coalition for Marriage's national partners. The budget for Focus on the Family alone dwarfed the combined resources of the two major national gay organizations, the National Gay and Lesbian Task Force (NGLTF) and the Human Rights Campaign (HRC). Grassroots mobilization would be essential to overcome the money advantage of the opposition.

In early 2004, NGLTF and HRC jump-started that organizing effort by giving MassEquality the funds to hire Marty Rouse, a veteran of the marriage struggle in Vermont, as its first campaign director. Rouse began immediately to organize a disciplined political campaign, mobilizing constituents across the state. The rallying call of "mass equality" energized volunteers from diverse gay, civil rights, labor, and religious organizations, including the ACLU of Massachusetts, Parents and Friends of Lesbians and Gays, SEIU locals, and the more than six hundred members of the Religious Coalition for the Freedom to Marry. On February 10, three thousand marriage equality supporters jammed inside and crowded outside the State House to lobby and rally. They countered the Coalition for Marriage's message of "let the people vote" with their own: "The constitution—defend it, don't amend it."

HIGH ANXIETY IN THE LEGISLATURE

Legislators were torn. Constituents were impassioned and divided—and they were making their voices heard. It was going to be a difficult vote. Representative Steven Tolman expressed sentiments typical of many legislators: "Initially, thinking of two men united in marriage didn't sit well with me, I have to be honest. Being brought up a Catholic and having those values, I'm comfortable thinking of marriage as a man and a woman." But when a lesbian mother came to visit Tolman in his office, he began to waver. She told Tolman that on November 18, the day of the court decision, "I actually felt equal."

Don't get me wrong, I love my marriage, but it feels like I drank from a Whites' Only fountain.

—Ben Atherton-Zeman,
a heterosexual advocate
of same-sex marriage

Marty Rouse (right), campaign director for
MassEquality, with his partner, Scott Sherman,
and their son, Sasha.

Tolman was practically brought to tears. "She was so sincere. It made it even more difficult for me," he explained.

THE 2004 CONSTITUTIONAL CONVENTIONS

The marble halls, the finely wrought furnishings, the historic murals, the aura of history that emanates from every inch of the State House usually seems much more majestic than the mundane business conducted there. Fast gaveling, a wink and a nod, backslapping, and arcane parliamentary procedures often leave the ordinary citizen lost in any attempt to follow a piece of legislation. Moments of genuine thoughtfulness, soul-searching, and stirring eloquence occur infrequently. Opportunities to extend justice and equality in a very broad sense are rare in the day-to-day work of legislators. But as the citizens of the commonwealth and the world would soon discover, given the opportunity, twenty-first-century legislators could rise to levels of eloquence, insightfulness, and passion equaling that of their predecessors whose words and austere portraits surround them.

Notably, as legislators embarked on this twenty-first-century debate concerning the constitutional rights of their gay and lesbian constituents, something was different. People of color, women, and openly gay legislators were speaking from the podium. Involved in multiple civil rights struggles in their lifetimes, they would play a pivotal role by turning a debate regarding people's feelings about homosexuality, marriage, morality, and religion into one about constitutional freedoms, civil rights, justice, and equality. They would push their colleagues to ask themselves two fundamental questions: first, "What role does religious doctrine have in defining the laws of civil society?" and second, "Is it fair to have the people vote on the rights of a minority?" In formulating their answers, during four full days of debate—February 11 and 12 and March 11 and 29—legislators would elevate the conversation and evoke the respect and pride of the electorate.

The only God that I know from my studying of scripture is a god of justice, a god who demands that every single person have the rights that they need to flourish and live in society.

—Bishop M. Thomas Shaw, Episcopal Diocese of Eastern Massachusetts

Octavio Delgado, a same-sex marriage supporter, shows his patriotism while others nearby wave the rainbow flag, a symbol of the
gay and lesbian civil rights movement.

Opponents of same-sex marriage hit the sidewalks outside the State House to deliver their message.

The Call to Order

February 11, 2004, the first day of the constitutional convention, was a crisp New England winter day. Blue skies and sunshine took some of the curse off the cold. Busloads of religious conservatives, many from out of state, arrived at the State House beginning at seven that morning, bearing signs with slogans like REMEMBER SODOM AND GOMMORAH, 1 MAN + 1 WOMAN = MARRIAGE, LET THE PEOPLE VOTE, and GOT AIDS YET? Pro-equality supporters, buoyed by the SJC's decision for gay marriage, brandished signs with their own slogans: THE CONSTITUTION—DEFEND IT—DON'T AMEND IT, NO DISCRIMINATION IN THE CONSTITUTION, SEPARATE IS NOT EQUAL. By 7:30 a.m., hundreds of people were lined up to get one of the 120 seats in the State House gallery open to the public.

In the corridors of the State House and outside on Beacon Street, chants broke out: "Let the people vote" counterpointed by "Equality now." Chants of "Jesus, Jesus, Jesus" were co-opted by the equality side, who punctuated every "Jesus" with "loves us." Inside the State House, for almost twelve straight hours the equality forces sang "God Bless America," "The Star-Spangled Banner," "We Shall Not Be Moved," "America the Beautiful," "We Shall Overcome"—in short, every patriotic and civil rights anthem known to the crowd. Anti–gay marriage forces kneeled, praying aloud, or stood with outstretched arms as if to exorcise the demons of the pro-equality forces gathered around them. Variations on this scene would be repeated during the four meetings of the 2004 constitutional convention. By giving witness, the swell of demonstrators would become critical to influencing legislators and attracting nonstop media coverage.

By noon, when senate president Robert Travaglini, the presiding officer of the constitutional convention, gaveled the body to order, all of the legislators had heard the singing and seen the crowds. Travaglini set the tone for the proceedings against patriotic refrains. "This is the essence of democracy. . . . Today we will be doing serious work concerning our constitution, the oldest in America. We intend to debate these issues in a responsible, dignified, and

Andy Mallon, wearing a button that said HI! I'M A SECOND-CLASS GAY CITIZEN, and his partner, John Olsen, joined thousands who lined the halls of the State House to express their views on same-sex marriage.

orderly manner." Travaglini had barely finished talking when Speaker of the House Thomas Finneran asked for a brief recess and, departing from the plan he had previously agreed to, requested the courtesy of being allowed to make some opening remarks.

The Speaker's Surprise Amendment

Finneran, a master of parliamentary procedure, shocked Travaglini and his colleagues by introducing a surprise amendment, a DOMA, limiting marriage to one man and one woman. The day before, Travaglini, a Democrat, had announced that he and Republican leader Brian Lees would introduce a more palatable DOMA amendment that would define marriage as the union of one man and one woman but that would also explicitly create civil unions for same-sex partners. This carefully worded, separate but equal compromise was intended to give legislators a chance to have it both ways: to support traditional marriage but give same-sex couples all the rights and benefits of marriage. It was the amendment members expected to debate. Finneran's amendment, by contrast, gave the legislature the authority to create civil unions but deferred action to "sometime in the near future."

Finneran's draconian move thrilled conservatives but violated the spirit of open debate urged by Travaglini. By the rules of the legislature, a favorable vote on the Finneran amendment meant that there could be no discussion or vote on the Travaglini-Lees amendment, and, once again, family recognition for gay men and lesbians would be shunted off to another day.

With Finneran's amendment on the floor, debate began. Over the next three hours, supporters of the Speaker argued that the supreme judicial court overstepped its bounds; that Mother Nature, not the SJC, defined marriage; and that the people should be given the opportunity to vote on "redefining" marriage. Representative David Flynn summed up the arguments in favor: "This is not . . . about civil rights. It's not about civil law. It's about natural law with me, the law of nature. The supreme judicial court can and does

Facing page, top
Protesters from both sides of the same-sex marriage debate jockey for hallway space in the State House.

Facing page, bottom
Brendan Curran, along with other marriage equality advocates, uses an enormous U.S. flag to attest to his patriotism and devotion to the Massachusetts constitution.

As religious conservatives kneel in prayer, marriage equality supporters surround them with their own messages.

invoke the law of man. The supreme judicial court cannot repeal the law of nature. . . . My only message is to let the people vote."

Prior to the meeting of the constitutional convention, fifty of the two hundred legislators had committed to supporting marriage equality and full civil rights for gay men and lesbians. As they rose to speak, these pro-equality legislators passionately defended the constitutional rights of all citizens. They hammered home an argument that would be heard over and over throughout the convention—the constitution should not be used to discriminate. As Senator Harriette Chandler insisted, "Our constitution has stood for equality for over two hundred years. This amendment is inconsistent with these principles. . . . The issue before us is whether to adopt an amendment that bars a segment of society rights afforded to others."

African American senator Diane Wilkerson referenced the parallel struggle blacks had endured not fifty years ago. Born in Arkansas during Jim Crow, she shared the pain that continues to haunt her: "I know firsthand that world of almost being equal. I could not in good conscience ever vote to send anyone to that place from where my family fled."

Emotions ran high as legislators argued over their understandings of marriage and family and their commitment to constitutional principles of liberty and freedom. Several legislators took the brave step of rebuking the powerful and vindictive Speaker for introducing a surprise amendment. Minority leader Senator Brian Lees, who had been expected to make the opening remarks before Finneran took the podium, declared, "What happened a few moments ago absolutely shocked me." Lees reminded his colleagues that for years the senate had sent to the house domestic-partnership and civil-union bills that Speaker Finneran had blocked.

To the great relief of the lesbian and gay community and its allies the Finneran amendment went down three votes short of the 101 needed for adoption. The victory, however, was tempered by the realization that 98 senators and representatives had voted for a measure that not only would have overturned the *Goodridge* decision but also did not guarantee any form

No change to the constitution of our commonwealth or this nation should ever be used to limit the rights of its citizens or we risk becoming the force that our founding fathers fought so bravely to defeat.

—*Representative Marty Walsh*

Arline Isaacson walks through the State
House, conferring with Mary Bonauto and communications consultant Mary Breslauer on a
voting strategy.

of family recognition for lesbians and gay men. Of the hundred legislators who had voted against the amendment, approximately half were pro-equality forces committed to defending *Goodridge* and half were those who preferred a civil-unions compromise.

With only about fifty legislators solidly in the pro-equality camp, building a majority against amending the constitution would take forceful lobbying and inventive strategizing. The pro-equality lobby team, led by Arline Isaacson and Bill Conley of the Massachusetts Gay and Lesbian Political Caucus and Norma Shapiro and Ann Lambert of the American Civil Liberties Union, huddled with pro-equality legislators and other gay and lesbian leaders to identify potential allies and parliamentary maneuvers to stave off defeat.

A Potential Compromise Fails

With Finneran's amendment disposed of, legislators immediately turned to the next challenge, the Travaglini-Lees separate but equal compromise. Conservatives disliked the amendment because of its guarantee of civil unions. Marriage equality supporters also lined up against the amendment because it excluded same-sex partners from marriage. For many legislators, however, it was the fig leaf they were looking for—a way to offer same-sex couples expanded rights and benefits without having to cast a vote for same-sex marriage.

For the next five hours, the emotional debate continued. The arguments were broadcast across the state by cable news and streamed live on computers; legislators were speaking not only to their colleagues but to everyone in the commonwealth. Among those who opposed any form of relationship recognition, the amendment was what Representative Stephen Tobin called "a poison pill." He forcefully argued that the measure was irrational: "You are voting against gay marriage but at the same time putting into the constitution some measures for gay unions. When it gets to the ballot, it will fail. It will. And you will be left with same-sex marriage, by default." Tobin and his pro-DOMA allies felt it was unfair and unwise to ask citizens to vote on same-sex marriage and civil unions in the same ballot question. They continued to push for an amendment that would simply define marriage as "the union of one man and one woman."

Marriage equality supporters were equally passionate about defeating the separate but equal compromise but for different reasons. Representative Marie St. Fleur, a fervent Catholic of Haitian descent, told her audience that "you can't compromise on discrimination." Calling herself the poster child for groups who have faced injustice, she proclaimed that "but for the equal protections of the laws, I would not enjoy the position of freedom I have today."

Senator Brian Joyce reminded his colleagues of the historic significance of judicial decisions in expanding civil rights. "I am unconvinced that civil rights should be decided at the ballot box, when emotions are so inflamed. Had the ban on interracial marriage or the decision segregating schools been put on the ballot, each may have been overturned. That does not mean those decisions were wrong."

But for many, the amendment offered an appropriate compromise. Senator Marc Pacheco rose in support: "We have a compromise proposal that does three things: first, it preserves the definition of marriage as one man and one woman. Second, it takes care of the interests of existing people who already have rights accrued to them [through employer-based domestic partnership] and affords them in the future. Third, it gives the citizens a voice and a vote." This, concluded Pacheco, is what the "mainstream average citizen is saying" he wants.

Pacheco, like many of his colleagues, felt uneasy about defending same-sex marriage, but at the same time he and others did not want to vote against equal rights. This group of legislators hoped that the separate but equal compromise would ensure that their gay and lesbian constituents finally received some form of family recognition while also satisfying their constituents who were demanding a vote on same-sex marriage. It was the path of least resistance, particularly in the face of upcoming elections.

Representative Marie St. Fleur, with Representative Shaun Kelly and Representative Liz Malia directly behind her, joins constituents in the crowded State House. Behind them are (L-R) Representative Byron Rushing, Representative Mike Festa, and MGLPC lobbyist Bill Conley.

Thus it came as a surprise when, late in the evening, a vote on the Travaglini-Lees amendment fell seven votes short of the 101 needed for adoption. Though 94 legislators favored the middle-of-the-road separate but equal amendment, they were outnumbered by the combined 104 votes of conservatives holding out for an uncompromised DOMA and the marriage equality supporters who were against any amendment at all. At 9 p.m., after seven hours with no action taken, the constitutional convention recessed until noon the next day.

The Soul-Searching Deepens

As they listened to their constituents, their churches, and their colleagues, many legislators struggled with making the right decision. Representative Doug Petersen, who became a champion of equal marriage, later recounted his own process.

Petersen shared his office with Representative Byron Rushing, an African American and longtime champion of civil rights. Petersen wondered out loud one day, "Why are same-sex couples insisting on marriage? What's the difference if we give them civil unions, with all the same rights and benefits?" Rushing responded, "Doug, if we said to African Americans, you can have all the rights and benefits of marriage, but we're going to call it civil unions, how would you vote?" Petersen got it—civil unions could never be equal. They would consign gay and lesbian families to a permanent second-class status. He never turned back.

Others were moved by the openly gay and lesbian legislators who had become their colleagues and friends. Conservative Republican representative Shaun Kelly, who sat near Representative Liz Malia, a Democrat and an open lesbian, in the house chamber, emerged as an eloquent ally. On the second day of the constitutional convention, Kelly rose to speak and began, "Liz, this is for you." Addressing his colleagues, Kelly noted, "Enshrining in a constitution, a sacred document, a notion that when [Liz] leaves this chamber . . . she doesn't have the privilege that other people have . . . cannot possibly jibe with

Facing page
Senator Diane Wilkerson, a marriage equality supporter, acknowledges the crowd's cheer of thanks. Other legislators who spoke eloquently for the marriage equality cause are standing in the crowd (L-R): Kathi-Anne Reinstein, Ellen Story, Alice Wolf, Doug Petersen, Gloria Fox, Byron Rushing, and Cory Atkins.

what the constitution and democracy is all about." He then personalized his argument further. "If you believe that the love Liz has for her partner is less than the love that you have for your spouse, I would suggest that you are wrong. I think that's really what this is about, the judgment of love and the importance of it." Kelly's speech left numbers of legislators in tears, but his motion to adjourn and leave the constitution intact failed.

Senator Jarrett Barrios, an openly gay legislator, pointed out that he and his partner of ten years, Doug Hattaway, and their two sons would be deeply affected if the constitution was amended to take away the rights that had finally been granted to them by the SJC. Barrios told the legislators that when his seven-year-old son was ill with a 104.5-degree fever, Barrios had called a nurse, who, rather than dealing with his child's illness, challenged his parental authority since Doug Hattaway was listed as the child's father. Barrios underscored the dilemma of many gay and lesbian people in dealing with the medical establishment: "I thought [my son] could die on my watch while I was fighting with a nurse over whether I was his parent or not." The denial of medical decision powers and hospital visitation rights struck a chord for everyone.

Representative Malia also spoke personally of the impact of a DOMA amendment on her and her partner: "If I were to die, my partner of thirty years might lose her home, our home that we have worked for and paid for, because she would have to pay an incredible inheritance tax. I ask you, please, look into your hearts. . . . Do not carve in stone a status less than equal."

Marriage advocate Evan Wolfson's prediction that debating marriage equality would "make it easier for nongay people to understand who we are" was coming true. Marriage was something that most legislators took for granted. They understood both its psychological and tangible benefits. Now they were beginning to see how the denial of civil-marriage rights for same-sex couples not only undermined the security of families but carried the message that gay men and lesbians were less than equal.

Blurring the Separation of Church and State

From the beginning, the opposition to same-sex marriage was cast almost entirely in faith-based terms. With the Catholic Church leading this faith-based lobbying effort, local parishes became ground zero for swaying public opinion against same-sex marriage. Huge televisions appeared at Masses to screen *Same-Sex Marriage: Truth or Consequences*, a deceptive video condemning gay and lesbian families. One million brochures attacking marriage equality arrived in the mailboxes of the faithful. Sermons purposefully confused the religious sacrament of marriage with civil marriage sanctioned by the state. Church leaders misled parishioners into believing that churches would be required by law to marry same-sex couples. In addition, the Catholic leadership directly lobbied Catholic legislators, who made up 67 percent of the membership.

Some legislators were loath to defy the teachings of the Church, but others found the Church leadership, who were embroiled in the clergy sexual abuse scandal, disingenuous. Archbishop Sean O'Malley spoke with freshman representative Steven Walsh for forty minutes on the phone. But Walsh's faith led him to reject his church's official position: "As a Catholic my faith tells me I must fight for the equality of all." Walsh paid homage to a hero of his, a priest who marched in Selma with Martin Luther King, Jr.: "I prefer to think of Father MacDonald's church, a church that used its influence to stop oppression and discrimination, not foster it." Representative Walsh and numbers of other legislators remembered that as public leaders, they swore on the Bible to uphold the constitution—not the other way around.

*O*rganized Catholicism is poised for jihad . . . against the State Supreme Judicial Court's decision to end discrimination in marriage.

—*Margery Eagan*,
Boston Herald *columnist*

Using Senator Jarrett Barrios's office as a refuge from the crowds, FTMC advocacy director Josh Friedes and GLAD interim director Margaret Williams (rear) tune in to the constitutional convention debate.

Openly gay legislators Jarrett Barrios (far left)
and Liz Malia (center) confer in the State House
hallway with a colleague as members of the
media look on.

Facing page, top
Pam Johnson of the MASS Black LGBT Alliance holds "Marriage Is a Civil Rights Issue," a document that the organization gave to all state legislators asking for their support in preserving marriage equality. Surrounding Johnson are (L-R) Douglas Brooks, Judah Dorrington, Jacquie Bishop, Letta Neely, and Gary Daffin (cochair of MGLPC).

Facing page, bottom
Marriage equality opponents, believing that homosexuality is a sin, express their opposition to civil unions as well as same-sex marriage.

Citizens Get into the Act

With the Super Tuesday Democratic presidential primaries scheduled for March 2, 2004, legislators waited a month before they took up marriage equality again. On primary day, six hundred MassEquality volunteers assigned to polling places across the state asked voters to sign postcards urging their legislators to oppose any amendment banning same-sex marriage. The campaign was a huge success. Two days later, MassEquality launched a series of thirty-second TV spots that asserted "Civil unions are not equal. Don't put discrimination in our constitution."

March rallies brought together different constituencies, including faith-based organizations and the children of lesbian and gay families, to speak out in favor of same-sex marriage. And in an event that made headlines and captured prime-time news slots throughout the state, World Wrestling Federation personality and former Minnesota governor Jesse Ventura and state auditor and former boxing champion Joe DeNucci held a press conference at the State House to show that "real men" favored marriage equality.

When the constitutional convention reconvened on March 11, huge crowds converged on the State House. Across the front of the capitol, a forty-foot-long fluorescent orange banner proclaiming JESUS IS THE LORD begged the question of separation of church and state. A half hour before the convention began, with nearly four thousand people already inside, state police closed off the building to anyone else. Another fifteen hundred people on both sides of the issue stood and chanted in front of the State House. Three Crucifixion reenactors shouldered full-size crosses as they paced before crowds. Individual debates and chanting matches filled the air. "Ho, ho, homosexuals have got to go." "One man, one woman, let the people vote." "Defend the constitution." "Sodomite, sodomite, sodomite." "Separate is unequal."

Across the front of the State House on the morning of March 11, 2004, when the constitutional convention reconvened, opponents to same-sex marriage unfurled a forty-foot fluorescent orange banner proclaiming JESUS IS THE LORD.

Top
As crowds chanted, sang, and even prayed outside the State House, marriage equality supporters and opponents often engaged in "discussions."

Bottom
Former Minnesota governor Jesse "The Body" Ventura spoke out in favor of same-sex marriage.

Compromising Civil Rights

The marriage equality lobbyists realized that the key to protecting the constitution lay with the pro-DOMA conservatives who did not want to vote for civil unions. If the conservatives lined up with the marriage equality legislators against a newly proposed separate but equal compromise, the amendment might be defeated. But first, marriage equality legislators would have to be willing to cast strategic votes in favor of the compromise to ensure that it—and not a strict DOMA without a civil-unions guarantee—moved forward to a final vote.

To improve communication during this complex maneuver, on March 11 the lobby team distributed beepers to pro-marriage equality legislators. Using the beepers and their carefully thought out voting strategy, they succeeded in advancing the compromise amendment to a final reading on March 29.

In the final hours of the debate, Catholic senator Marion Walsh once again reiterated the importance of maintaining the separation of church and state: "I ask, what constitutional right would individuals . . . participating in religious activities like to give up? Would individuals who worship surrender their own religion, and enjoy a state religion? Would individuals who are clergy like to give up the authority to perform marriage ceremonies that this very legislature gave them in 1692?"

Walsh, like a number of her colleagues, admitted that she felt the *Goodridge* decision "is ahead of our mainstream culture. It's ahead of my own sensibilities." But having thought deeply about her role as a public leader, Walsh concluded, "My level of comfort is not the appropriate monitor for the constitutional rights of my constituents."

The last words before the vote came from Representative Liz Malia. "No matter the outcome, the movement for civil rights for all will move forward today and the next day and the day after. If you choose to tell us we are not equal I don't go away. We all don't go away. We will still raise our families. We will care for the elders in our community. We will sit beside you and work together with you but we will never give up the fight to be recognized as full equal human beings, citizens of this state and of this country."

The final vote was 105–92. The separate but equal compromise amendment, defining marriage as the union of one man and one woman and guaranteeing civil unions, had squeaked by. Malia later reflected that when the vote was announced there was no cheering, only an eerie silence in the chamber as legislators drifted out. Both sides were disappointed with the amendment. One political commentator likened it to a shotgun marriage. The shred of good news, though, was that the ranks of the pro-equality legislators had increased from fifty to at least seventy-seven of those ninety-two votes against the amendment. Those seventy-seven legislators made strange bedfellows with the fifteen radical DOMA supporters who could not abide granting civil unions—the poison pill.

We want every legislator to be held accountable for the vote they take in this very historic matter. . . . If people vote to take our rights away, they'll have to explain why they did it—this year, next year, five and ten years from now.

—*Arline Isaacson*

Top

GLAD attorney Mary Bonauto addressed the crowd at the March 10, 2004, MassEquality candlelight vigil. Representative Byron Rushing, a longtime supporter of the gay community and a leader on the same-sex marriage issue, is standing next to her.

Bottom

The RCFM and the National Religious Leadership Roundtable for LGBT Equality sponsored this interfaith event called As Long As You Both Shall Live: People of Faith Say Yes to Same-Sex Marriage, at the Emmanuel Church. In the foreground is the Reverend Carlton Smith, a Unitarian Universalist minister who was a leader in promoting marriage equality; Rabbi Devon Lerner, RCFM's executive director, is at the lectern.

Kate Brodoff, fifteen, daughter of Goodridge plaintiffs Maureen Brodoff and Ellen Wade, speaks at the Family Rally for Same-Sex Marriage at the Massachusetts State House.

*T*he Supreme Judicial Court's decision to permit same-gender marriage makes me feel proud to be an American, to live in a country that strives to guarantee everyone's religious freedom and civil rights.

—*Rabbi Devon Lerner, executive director of RCFM*

Facing page
The RCFM held many interfaith celebrations endorsing same-sex marriage. Rabbi Ronne Friedman, senior rabbi at Boston's Temple Israel, is speaking at the podium of Boston's Old South Church.

Throughout the meetings of the constitutional convention, parents turned out to support their children's right to marry.

Deb Cebulski was one of many who defied the stereotype that Catholics were against marriage equality.

At a Stop Same-Sex Marriage rally at Faneuil
Hall, Sarah Beth Skidmore, a passerby, argues in
favor of same-sex marriage with a man from a
conservative religious group.

(L-R): FTMC advocacy director Josh Friedes, Arline Isaacson, conservative MFI president Ron Crews (partial view), a member of the press, and ACLU lobbyist Norma Shapiro crowd around a monitor to watch a vote tally in the legislature.

Marriage equality supporters Alex Westerhoff and Tom Lang spent twelve hours at the State House singing patriotic songs and hoping to convince legislators that they should not amend the constitution to take away the right to marry. The supportive heterosexual couple beside them also stayed for twelve hours.

Jeannette and Ali Wicks-Lim bore witness and
sang for twelve hours to protect their right to
a civil marriage.

LAST-DITCH EFFORTS TO STOP SAME-SEX MARRIAGE FAIL

Unhappy with the compromise in the legislature, DOMA supporters nonetheless sought to use the amendment to their advantage to stop same-sex couples from receiving marriage licenses. Mary Bonauto documented that between March 29 and May 14, GLAD "faced a coordinated legal assault by a variety of public and private parties to stop marriages from happening as scheduled on May 17, 2004." It was not until 6 p.m. on May 14, just thirty hours before Cambridge would begin accepting the first applications for same-sex marriage licenses, that Bonauto learned that the U.S. Supreme Court had turned back the final challenge.

The lesbian and gay community breathed a deep sigh of relief and began planning for a flurry of spring weddings. The parties kicked off on Sunday afternoon, May 16, outside Cambridge City Hall, where couples lined up to apply for the marriage licenses that would be issued beginning at midnight on May 17. Massachusetts's week-long wedding party had begun (see chapter 4).

Throughout the remainder of the week, same-sex couples and their children dominated every news cycle. The positive public spirit that enveloped the entire state seemed immune to the negative predictions of marriage opponents, who forecast the end of civilization as we know it. The equal marriage struggle was far from over, but the playing field had shifted; with same-sex couples in every community in the state publicly declaring their love, it was becoming increasingly difficult to cast them in the role of enemy citizens.

ELECTIONS 2004

DOMA Supporters Seek to Shore Up Support in Next Legislature

Election season began just ten days after the first same-sex couples married. On May 27, with a great deal of fanfare, Governor Romney presented 121 Republican candidates for the fall legislative races in 200 districts—far more Republicans running for office than ever before. The governor, hoping to use

Facing page
May 17, 2004: Sue Hyde, an NGLTF organizer and a member of the MassEquality board, is all smiles on the first day of marriage equality. Pictured on the front page of the *Boston Globe* are Marcia Hams (center) and Susan Shepherd (right), the first same-sex couple to apply for a marriage license.

the marriage equality debate to significantly increase his party's representation in the traditionally Democratic-dominated state legislature, donated $3 million to support their campaigns. Though the marriage issue was not strictly partisan, the majority of new Republican candidates were expected to support the governor in his opposition to same-sex marriage.

In June, the Catholic Church entered the election fray. Vowing retaliation at the ballot box against legislators who supported marriage equality, the Church sent letters to its 710 parishes, targeting legislators who were "opposed to letting the people vote" on an amendment to ban same-sex marriage. Freshman representative Barbara L'Italien was forced to resign from her position as parish choir director because of her public support for marriage equality.

MassEquality Flexes Its Muscles

To counter these efforts, MassEquality and the Massachusetts Freedom to Marry Coalition, pledging to reelect the seventy-seven pro-equality legislators, kicked off their Summer of Equality. They recruited volunteers in every part of the state to support the campaigns of key allies, some of whom were fighting opponents for the first time in years. They also sent canvassers to targeted districts across the state to identify pro–marriage equality voters who would let their legislators know they supported gay marriage. At the June Pride Parade, which attracted the largest crowds in its thirty-four-year history, a voter registration drive kicked into high gear.

On September 14, as the primary results came in, MassEquality's campaign director Marty Rouse and political director Marc Solomon had much to celebrate. Emblematic of MassEquality's political success was Carl Sciortino's stunning victory in the Democratic primary over incumbent Vinny Ciampa, who had represented Somerville and Medford for years.

Sciortino, a twenty-five-year-old gay man, had been angered by Ciampa's opposition to same-sex marriage and his indifference toward social and economic justice issues. Rouse's dogged determination to protect legislative allies

Before the 2004 election, a vote for marriage equality for many legislators was a vote to defeat themselves.

—Marc Solomon, political director of MassEquality

Representative Sal DiMasi, elected house majority leader in 2004, with ACLU lobbyist Norma Shapiro and MGLPC cochair Arline Isaacson and unseat marriage equality opponents paid off. Incumbent and pro-gay candidates rolled to victory.

Almost immediately, marriage equality forces were blessed with good fortune matching their hard work. House Speaker Tom Finneran, who had so deeply offended his colleagues with his DOMA amendment at the February 2004 constitutional convention, became embroiled in a scandal over redistricting and was forced to resign. The new house leader, Representative Sal DiMasi, had been a longtime friend of the gay community, voting for gay civil rights since his first term, back in 1983. Finneran's departure, DiMasi's ascension, and the indictment on two charges of child rape of one of the most virulently anti-gay marriage Catholic bishops sent the same-sex marriage opposition reeling.

On November 2, 2004, as eleven states passed constitutional amendments prohibiting same-sex marriage, Massachusetts proved that the reality of gay people tying the knot was far less threatening to voters than the abstract possibility. Every pro-equality legislator was returned to office, and the vast majority of new candidates who had campaigned on pro–marriage equality platforms, including Carl Sciortino, replaced DOMA supporters. In total the Republicans lost three seats in the legislature—despite the governor's $3 million bounty. MassEquality had built the electoral machine that Rouse knew it needed. "Legislators would stick with us on the marriage issue," he said, "because we had become a politically powerful movement. They knew that it was going to cost them at the ballot box if they voted against us."

Though everyone seemed to want to blame the gay marriage issue for John Kerry's defeat in the presidential election, Bonauto and Rouse argued that such an analysis was simplistic and flawed. They pointed out that "62 percent of Americans left the polls favoring some sort of relationship recognition, from marriage to civil unions to domestic partnership." In Massachusetts, they noted, "voters have had the opportunity to live beside their newly married gay neighbors, and by and large, they have come to realize that marriage equality does not threaten them."

Freshman legislator John Keenan (far left), who had campaigned on a pro–marriage equality platform, brought his constituents Bob Murch and Gary Halteman, the first same-sex couple to marry in his Salem district, to meet with House Speaker Sal DiMasi (second from left).

Carl Sciortino celebrates his victory against
incumbent state representative Vinny Ciampa. In
the background, Sue Hyde and Marty Rouse show
their delight in Sciortino's victory.

Marc Solomon, political director of MassEquality, announces the primary victories before a cheering crowd of election volunteers gathered at Club Cafe.

POINT-COUNTERPOINT 2005

As same-sex marriage rounded the corner of its first anniversary, the opposition was finding it harder and harder to convince the people of Massachusetts that allowing loving same-sex couples and their families to benefit from civil marriage would result in anything but stronger and healthier communities. Nonetheless, opponents continued to look for ways to overturn the *Goodridge* decision or, if that was not possible, to limit its impact.

The governor and the attorney general stood by their decision to enforce a moribund 1913 law denying out-of-state couples the right to marry in Massachusetts if that marriage would not be legal in their home state. Governor Romney, seeking to enhance his conservative image nationally, also denied a request of the Massachusetts Town Clerks' Association "to create a new birth certificate for the children of same-sex parents that would include gender-neutral nomenclature." Despite the protests of the clerks that "cross-outs on birth certificates could make them open to challenges by passport agents, foreign governments, and other officials," Romney advised hospitals to "cross out the word 'father' . . . and instead write the phrase 'second parent.'"

These petty attacks did not deter marriage equality supporters, who quietly continued their lobbying throughout the spring and summer of 2005. According to MassEquality's Marc Solomon, legislators were invited to the homes of newly married couples in their districts. Several same-sex couples, often with children, would be present to explain how marriage had affected their lives. Many legislators also attended same-sex weddings of friends, colleagues, and constituents, where they experienced firsthand the overwhelming joy of Massachusetts lesbian and gay families.

ACLU lobbyist Norma Shapiro's strategy of "listening to find out what's keeping legislators from being on my side" worked in its low-key, persistent way. "I spoke with one opposing legislator with a gay brother who broke down crying. He thought he would lose in the next election. I listened. It wasn't what I said that brought him around." Shapiro's resourcefulness is legendary. "I've gotten a legislator's third-grade teacher to come in and talk with him."

Shapiro, with Arline Isaacson and Bill Conley of the MGLPC, launched "what they jokingly referred to as the 'sibling project.'" They sought out gay siblings and children of legislators to convince their relatives to vote against the amendment. During the legislative summer recess, they drove "siblings" to places far and wide in the state to meet legislators. "We didn't want to leave any stone unturned," declared Isaacson.

Having time to reflect and meet with constituents as well as seeing how meaningful marriage was to the same-sex couples who had taken advantage of their new civil rights, convinced many legislators to announce that when the constitutional convention met again in the fall of 2005, they would vote against the separate but equal amendment. Representative Anthony Petrucelli, who had voted for the amendment in 2004, told *Bay Windows*, "[*Goodridge*] has made stronger unions among people who have not had the opportunity up until that time to get married." He questioned, "Who am I to take away something from someone that they cherish?" After a year of same-sex weddings, Petrucelli concluded that civil unions would be "a major step backwards in equality."

As MassEquality used their grassroots troops to build a solid majority for marriage equality—and against amending the constitution—DOMA supporters were quietly abandoning the separate but equal compromise as well. In July 2005, they announced a campaign for a citizens' initiative that could put a new DOMA amendment—with no civil-unions guarantee—on the ballot in 2008. In response, two marriage-equality supporters—one heterosexual, one gay—created a Web site called Know Thy Neighbor that promised to put online the names of all citizens who signed the initiative. Though considered controversial by some, this strategy sparked dialogue among neighbors who found themselves on opposite sides of the issue.

*C*onstitutions all over the world grant rights. They do not take them away.

—*Representative Doug Petersen*

As legislators prepare to vote at the September 2005 constitutional convention, MGLPC cochair Arline Isaacson, Log Cabin Republican president Patrick Guerriero, and MassEquality campaign director Marty Rouse consult outside the chamber.

Senate minority leader Brian Lees speaks to the press after announcing his opposition to the constitutional amendment he had sponsored in the 2004 legislative session.

At the September 2005 constitutional convention, two marriage supporters react with joy and tears at the announcement of the 157-39 vote defeating the constitutional amendment.

SWEET VICTORY, SEPTEMBER 2005

By the time legislators returned from their summer recess in September 2005, it appeared that the separate but equal compromise amendment might be doomed. To go to the ballot in 2006, it would need to garner at least 101 of the 200 legislative votes in the 2005 constitutional convention, scheduled for September 14.

On the day of the convention, marriage equality advocates dominated both the street outside the State House and the Great Hall inside where the proceedings would be televised. Despite the perfect weather, the crowds did not come close to the numbers of the previous year. With momentum moving toward marriage equality, DOMA supporters were pinning their hopes on their 2008 ballot initiative.

Senate minority leader Brian Lees, a sponsor of the separate but equal compromise amendment, led off the convention by explaining that he had received more than seven thousand letters, e-mails, and telephone calls from people in his district and from across the state and the nation. He had finally decided on the very day of the convention to oppose his own amendment. "Gay marriage has begun and life has not changed for the citizens of the commonwealth with the exception of those who can now marry who couldn't before." He went on, "This amendment was an appropriate measure of compromise a year ago but it is no longer today." Pro-equality forces in the Great Hall gasped in unison and then burst into cheers.

Within minutes, Lees briefly left the constitutional convention that was still in session. Escorted by MGLPC's Arline Isaacson and the president of the Log Cabin Republicans, Patrick Guerriero, Lees entered the Great Hall. The crowd exploded with applause and began chanting, "Thank you. Thank you." Everyone sensed the beginning of a sea change.

Freshman representative Carl Sciortino, whose election had in many ways been a turning point in the marriage equality struggle, had the final word: "At last year's constitutional convention I sat out in the gallery upstairs. I sat out there in the Great Hall watching on the monitors. I stood out on the streets

Aaron Toleos and Tom Lang launched a Web site,
Know Thy Neighbor, that published the names
of those who signed the anti-same-sex marriage
petition.

protesting, singing, crying, and hugging fellow members of the GLBT community who had come here and all of our straight allies that stood there side by side with us." Urging his colleagues to defeat the amendment, he observed, "It's not a pleasant feeling when you have your own elected representatives and senators sitting in this chamber debating your right to exist as a fully equal citizen of the commonwealth." Sciortino's speech roused the chamber and thrilled the people in the Great Hall.

Senator Therese Murray called the question, and marriage equality supporters achieved one of their finest victories, defeating the separate but equal compromise amendment, 157–39. Seventeen of the eighteen freshman legislators who had been voted into office since the last constitutional convention voted pro-equality—a referendum on how public opinion had changed in less than a year and a half. MassEquality had made its mark. Representative Rushing captured the spirit when he urged his colleagues "to reflect on that wonderful quote that Martin Luther King loved and probably learned here in Boston because it was really said first by Theodore Parker in this city. 'The arc of the moral universe is long but it bends toward justice.' Today we will be bending that arc toward justice."

Same-Sex Marriage: An Uncertain Future

Despite the legislative victory in 2005 and the unquestioned success of same-sex marriage in Massachusetts—with more than nine thousand couples tying the knot by November 2006—the opposition locally, as well as nationally, continued its assault. Locally, the Catholic Church and its allies in the Coalition for Marriage formed Vote on Marriage to mobilize support for their new DOMA amendment. In addition, the Catholic Church began another attack on gay families, announcing in February 2006 that Catholic Charities, despite the unanimous dissent of its board, would no longer place children in need of homes with same-sex parents. The chair and six board members resigned in March in protest of the Church's decision.

Across the country, in the summer of 2006, same-sex marriage opponents were buoyed by high court rulings in Washington and New York that argued that legislatures had legitimate reasons—in particular, heterosexual procreation—for limiting marriage to one man and one woman. Both state supreme courts ruled against same-sex couples who wished to exercise their fundamental right to marry the person of their choice. Ironically, in the fall of 2005, the California legislature had decided in favor of same-sex marriage, but the governor had vetoed the bill, arguing that the courts should decide. In Massachusetts, where both the courts *and* the legislature supported same-sex marriage as a fundamental civil right, the challenges persisted. With Governor Romney and Cardinal O'Malley leading the charge, the call to "let the people vote" continued, even though polls showed that the residents of Massachusetts overwhelmingly favored same-sex marriage.

Though the inevitable setbacks were painful, the news for same-sex couples was not all bad. A Pew Research Center national poll in March 2006 showed that opposition to same-sex marriage was rapidly diminishing across the country. In October, the New Jersey Supreme Court unanimously ruled that same-sex couples are entitled to all the rights and benefits of marriage. Though the court left it to the legislature to decide if those benefits should be granted under current marriage statutes, as in Massachusetts, or through parallel civil unions, it was a significant leap forward for lesbian and gay families. In another victory for same-sex couples, Arizona residents, in the November elections, defeated a constitutional amendment that would have banned legal recognition of any relationships other than heterosexual marriage.

In the 2006 Massachusetts election, voters replaced a virulently anti-equality governor with a strong marriage equality supporter, the state's first African American governor, Deval Patrick. Two days later, the Massachusetts legislature reconvened in constitutional convention. Citizens on both sides of the marriage issue gathered outside the State House, as their representatives once again took up the same-sex marriage issue—this time to vote on the DOMA amendment brought forward by the citizens' petition. In a parliamen-

Facing page
Representative Byron Rushing is surrounded by pro–marriage equality colleagues and the press following the marriage equality victory at the September 2005 constitutional convention. Pictured (L-R): Rep. Carl Sciortino; MassEquality campaign director Marty Rouse; FTMC advocacy director Josh Friedes; Sen. Ed Augustus; Rep. Linda Dorcena-Forry; Rep. Mike Festa; Rep. David Linsky; Rep. Doug Petersen; Sen. Diane Wilkerson; Sen. Mark Montigny; MGLPC cochair Arline Isaacson; and Sen. Harriette Chandler.

tary maneuver hailed as courageous by marriage equality advocates and underhanded by same-sex marriage opponents, the majority of legislators voted to recess until the last day of the legislative session, January 2, 2007, rather than take up the amendment.

In the final weeks of 2006, those opposed to same-sex marriage kept up the pressure and, finally, captured the votes they needed to keep their petition alive. As 2007 opened, the constitutional convention reconvened and gave initial approval to placing the DOMA amendment on the ballot. But the fight was not over. The legislature would have to pass the amendment again before it could go to the voters in 2008. A new year had begun, along with another chapter in the continuing struggle for same-sex marriage.

Today is a happy and proud day for the people of Massachusetts. The commonwealth of Massachusetts once again takes its place as a leader in this country in the fight for full and equal rights for all people.

—Senator Ed Augustus

Facing page
Massachusetts citizens celebrate the defeat of the anti–gay marriage amendment at the September 2005 constitutional convention. On the right are openly lesbian legislator Liz Malia and assistant majority leader Lida Harkins. Between them, in the back, is Senator Harriette Chandler. All three women spoke movingly in favor of marriage equality during the convention.

Keith Maynard and Chip McLaughlin, having filed
for a marriage license in the early hours of May
17, 2004, respond to the greetings of the jubilant
crowd outside of Cambridge City Hall.

HERE COME THE BRIDES,
HERE COME THE GROOMS

Celebrating Marriage Equality

Here come the brides. / So gay with pride. / Isn't it wondrous / They somehow survived.

—Song sung to Hillary and Julie Goodridge by their wedding guests

LOVE AND MARRIAGE

"Love and marriage, love and marriage, go together like a horse and carriage
. . ." or so the song says. Falling in love and marrying, the experiences that
are the themes of countless songs, poems, novels, films, and soap operas, never
came within the grasp of the lesbian and gay community in the United
States—that is, until Massachusetts made it possible. Of course couples fell in
love and committed to each other, but marrying—that step of standing before
the community and solemnizing a bond signifying responsibility, respect, and
privilege—*that* the lesbian and gay community could experience only vicari-
ously. No action a person takes in life symbolizes more than committing to
another person, but that rite of passage, building security for couples, stabi-
lizing communities, and affirming families, is legally denied to the vast majority of lesbians and gay men.

Denying people in love the right to marry has a long history as a way to
demean and denigrate. Those who enslaved African Americans in this country made sure that they "got religion" but still barred them from marriage,
religious or civil. Nazis tried to assure that the Aryan race would not be taint-
ed by intermarriage with Jews. Interracial marriages remained illegal in much
of the United States until 1967.

In this history of shame, however, Massachusetts has remained a beacon
of hope. In 1843 the Massachusetts legislature repealed a statute banning
interracial marriages. One hundred sixty years later, on November 18, 2003,
the Massachusetts SJC ruled that same-sex marriage was legal. In 2005, the
Massachusetts legislature, recognizing the importance of legal protections
for couples and families, overwhelmingly rejected an amendment to the state
constitution that would have banned same-sex couples from marrying. In
official testimony, legislators shared how touched they were by the love in lesbian and gay families. There always was love and then came marriage—in
Massachusetts. Cambridge led the way.

Facing page
Alex Fennell and Sasha Hartman
swore to the truth of their marriage license application before
Paula Crane, executive secretary
to the mayor of Cambridge.

As couples lined up to apply for marriage licenses
at Cambridge City Hall, love was in the air.

Alison Chase and the Reverend Marta Valentin wave to the cheering crowd as they leave Cambridge City Hall.

FREE TO MARRY, AT LAST—MAY 17, 2004

Susan Shepherd and Marcia Hams, a couple for twenty-seven years, proved to the world that wanting to have the first legal same-sex marriage license in the country meant that you'd do the extraordinary. Cambridge, a city well known for its progressive politics, would be the first municipality to open for business, at 12:01 a.m. on Monday, May 17. Susan secured the first place in line at Cambridge City Hall, and on Saturday, May 15, the longtime Cambridge residents tucked into sleeping bags under their big tarp close to the front door. The couple, along with their twenty-four-year-old son, Peter, is wild about sports, and so this made sense to Marcia: "If people can do this for Red Sox tickets, we certainly can do this for our lives."

On Sunday, more couples arrived to get in line. A family festival took shape on the sloping lawn of City Hall. Dogs and kids cavorted. Frisbees flew. Handstands and somersaults wowed the gathering crowds. Kids and adults played catch. Couples held hands and shared their wedding plans. Every once in a while people would pinch themselves, wondering if the bliss would last, if they'd really get marriage licenses, if there would really be a wedding for them.

At 10:30 p.m. on Sunday night, when Mayor Michael Sullivan invited couples into City Hall for music, speeches, and a champagne and cake reception, the crowd of supporters outside had swelled; by midnight, the media estimated the crowd had reached ten thousand. TV crews lit up the scene. The excitement built. Kids waved glow sticks. Everyone sensed history in the making. Inside, the Boston Women's Rainbow Chorus belted out "Going to the Chapel" and the Cambridge Chorus wowed the couples with the Beatles' hit "Can't Buy Me Love." When Mayor Sullivan said, "It is a day to celebrate the immense commitment that couples make to each other. . . . It is a day to recognize the commitment . . . of oneself to something greater than oneself," the couples cheered him on appreciatively.

The countdown to the first second of May 17 began inside and outside the building, and the city block rocked with cheers at 12:01 a.m. Within the hour, the first couples emerged, waving their completed white application cards to the wild applause of thousands. Reporters and TV crews pressed in. Well-wishers handed the couples roses, threw confetti and rice, and kept up spirited rounds of "Going to the Chapel," "God Bless America," and "America the Beautiful."

Shepherd, clutching the first fully legal U.S. marriage license application for a gay couple, told a reporter, "This is like winning the World Series and the Stanley Cup on the same day. I'm trying not to lose it. We just really feel awesome. It's awesome." Her partner, Hams, thinking of their son, Peter, an NCAA hockey star, looked into a TV camera and said, "There's a kid somewhere that's watching this. It's going to change his whole life."

While Shepherd and Hams had planned to be at Cambridge City Hall, Ralph Hodgdon and Paul McMahon, who had been together for almost forty-nine years, did not have marriage at the top of their agenda. That all changed, though, on Sunday, May 16, just after 11 p.m. As they watched the eleven-o'clock news they saw the huge crowds and exuberant party building at Cambridge City Hall. That was it. They rushed out and took the subway to the festivities, just to be supportive. Once at City Hall, they got swept up in the spirit. McMahon recalls, "We got there and the excitement was so wonderful, it was so positive and people were so supportive, the next thing you know we're in line."

When they emerged at five-thirty in the morning with their completed application, a crew from *Good Morning America* pounced on them. McMahon and Hodgdon became two of the new faces of commitment and love—and, soon, marriage. On May 29, 2004, looking very handsome in their tuxedoes, they celebrated their forty-ninth anniversary by getting married by a justice of the peace in the Boston Public Garden.

By the close of business on May 17, Cambridge topped the state in marriage applications, taking in 268, and then issuing licenses to couples who obtained court waivers on the usual three-day waiting period. Few failed to notice the incredible generosity of city workers, ranging from the superin-

After we got our Notice of Intention, we went up the stairs to go out the front door. When the door opened, lights were flashing and thousands of folks were cheering as if we were the Rolling Stones on a 1975 tour or something. That night, I had a glimpse of what it must be like to be famous and it was unbelievable on many levels. What resounded for me then and now is the love we felt from all of those people. It just got inside of us and we went down the front steps as if on a cloud—the feeling was surreal and profoundly indescribable.

—*Jennifer Hess*

tendent of schools to the chief public health officer to the city clerk's staff, who volunteered to stay up all night ushering in this historic era of marriage equality.

Cambridge was also the site of the first marriage when, shortly after 9 a.m., city clerk Margaret Drury married a couple that had been together for eighteen years. Tanya McCloskey and Marcia Kadish promised each other "my friendship, my support, my love." Media from around the world captured the moment. The two women, who up until then had led largely private lives, found themselves coming out to an international audience as a married couple. McCloskey, lost for words, choked out, "I'm so happy right now. This is a dream come true. To stand in front of all these people makes us nervous but proud." Kadish agreed: "I'm glowing from the inside. Happy is an understatement."

After they married, Ralph Hodgdon and Paul McMahon became an integral part of pro-marriage equality events, holding their annually updated sign.

Cambridge city clerk Margaret Drury with
Marcia Kadish and Tanya McCloskey

Peter Hams, with his mothers, Marsha Hams
and Susan Shepherd, the first same-sex couple
to apply for a Massachusetts marriage license.

Julie and Hillary Goodridge, accompanied by their daughter, Annie, register to marry at Boston City Hall. Mary Bonauto and Mayor Thomas Menino look on.

ALL THE PLAINTIFFS MARRY—MEDIA MADNESS

Across the river, couples, reporters, satellite trucks, and well-wishers began gathering on Boston's City Hall Plaza at 3 a.m. on May 17. The *Today* show, CNN, and the BBC set up shop. One couple that had never been interviewed before seemed overwhelmed in talking with "a newspaper from Spain, a television station from Japan, *People* magazine, NBC, NPR, Channel 7"—the world watched. Signs around the plaza declared, MARRIAGE IS A FUNDAMENTAL HUMAN RIGHT.

Mayor Thomas Menino rolled out the red carpet and attended to every detail to make May 17 a flawless and memorable day. The first licenses were reserved for three of the *Goodridge* plaintiff couples who had come to this same building three years before and been denied the licenses that they now had won—for everyone. Menino and Bonauto looked on approvingly as each of the plaintiffs filed a notice. The three couples then went to court, obtained waivers, came back to City Hall to cheering crowds, got their marriage licenses, and finally relaxed for a moment at a reception compliments of the city. Before the day was over, all of the plaintiff couples would marry.

Hillary and Julie

Hillary and Julie Goodridge married in a civil ceremony at the Unitarian Universalist Association (UUA) headquarters with their daughter, Annie, as ring bearer and flower girl. Hillary's UUA colleagues and the couple's friends serenaded them with "Here Come the Brides." The Reverend William Sinkford, UUA president, paid tribute to their groundbreaking struggle: "The legal case that will forever bear your name has been a gift, not just to the thousands of same-sex couples who will marry this week, but to all the residents of the Commonwealth. You have helped us expand yet again who we mean when we say, 'We the people.'"

Dave and Rob

David Wilson and Rob Compton, with their grown children present and the Boston Gay Men's Chorus singing their signature number, "Marry Us," were wed at the Arlington Street Church. When the Reverend Kim Crawford Harvie intoned the words, "By the power vested in me by the Commonwealth of Massachusetts," applause and cheers shook the venerable old church. When the uproar subsided she said, "I hereby pronounce you partners for life, legally married."

*I*t is the historic aspect of this that feels strange, pleasant, and disquieting. I keep ruminating on what it means to be "normal" versus "not normal"; "different" and "not different." I feel like I was a part of the dismantling of the Berlin Wall—the dismantling of something that was literally both concrete and ideological.

—*Evelyn Hammonds, reflecting on her marriage at the Arlington Street Church*

Dave Wilson and Rob Compton look on as the
Reverend Kim Crawford Harvie signs their
marriage license at the Unitarian Universalist
Arlington Street Church.

Ellen and Maureen

Ellen Wade and Maureen Brodoff married in the mayor's office at Newton City Hall. Close to five hundred community members, among them state legislators, city officials, and lots of families with kids, celebrated with the couple and their daughter, Kate. Brodoff, in a loving and wry gesture to her own parents who had married very young and whose marriage had flourished, said, "Ellen and I have waited twenty-four years to get married but let me tell you—not to disapprove of your choice to get married so young—waiting does have its advantages. You were young and foolish, but lucky enough to have become perfect mates for each other. Here there is no luck involved. I know exactly who it is that I'm marrying and this marriage is, for that reason, so much more precious."

Mike and Ed

Mike Horgan and Ed Balmelli, fearful up until the beginning of May that some court would stop gay marriage, hastily put together a very elegant wedding in less than two weeks and married at a Boston hotel. Massachusetts Freedom to Marry Coalition advocacy director Josh Friedes toasted the couple. "I guess the question that everybody is wondering is, how can you make the perfect day even more perfect? For me it's being present at my best friends' wedding on the day in which, for people like me, they achieved full civil rights for people like all of us."

Linda and Gloria

Out on Cape Cod, plaintiffs Linda Davies and Gloria Bailey got the license they'd been denied three years before. Gloria remembered how hard it had been to go down to Orleans Town Hall and ask the same clerk who granted her a dog license and a fishing and clamming license to give her a marriage license. "Gee, you go into town hall and joke with these folks and have that kind of relationship but then to ask for a marriage license knowing that we wouldn't get it—that was tough. The clerk felt bad, too. But three years later

Facing page
Massachusetts FTMC advocacy director Josh Friedes toasts Mike Horgan and Ed Balmelli at their wedding at the Boston Marriott, Copley Place.

we got a license." They married in a private ceremony on Nauset Beach, with Gloria promising a more elaborate affair in July with hundreds of guests. "We figure after thirty-three years we're entitled to two weddings."

Heidi and Gina

In the westernmost part of the state, hundreds of well-wishers at Northampton City Hall greeted plaintiffs Heidi Norton and Gina Smith. In seeking a waiver of the three-day waiting period, Heidi told the judge, "Your Honor, I have been in love with Gina since 1990." In a little park a short walk from their house, Heidi and Gina and their sons, Avery and Quinn, became the Nortonsmiths, and each began wearing a similar chain-link bracelet showing their connection. "I didn't ever dare hope for this day until last November," said Heidi's father, Perry Norton.

Gary and Rich

In the whole marriage whirlwind, the central Massachusetts city of Worcester played a key role. City clerk David Rushford, a Catholic, was attacked by the bishop of the diocese for speaking out in favor of allowing out-of-state same-sex couples to marry in Massachusetts. But even the bishop could not dampen the joy of the day or Rushford's commitment to equal rights and the separation of church and state. On May 17, Rushford welcomed all couples. The first license went to plaintiffs Rich Linnell and Gary Chalmers.

In an evening candlelight ceremony in their packed family church with their daughter, Paige, at their side, the last plaintiff couple married. Their minister, who for one year had refused to sign any licenses for heterosexual couples until same-sex couples could marry, acknowledged the achievement of the men. "I believe we study history or make history. We're grateful to Rich and Gary and Paige for the history they made for thousands of couples that can finally be recognized as legitimate in the Commonwealth."

MASSACHUSETTS OPENS ITS HEART

The week of May 17 was a remarkable time. Each day, in communities across the commonwealth, people opened their local newspapers to pictures of rejoicing couples with children, family, and friends, celebrating equality, justice, and love. With the joyful spirit of weddings tugging at their hearts, few wanted to rain on the parade of so many people publicly demonstrating their love.

On May 17, town clerks in the far corners of the state opened their offices early to welcome couples who often had waited years for this moment. On the first day of marriage equality, more than a thousand same-sex couples streamed in to apply for marriage licenses. They were greeted with flowers and cookies and lots of hugs from well-wishers. In the tiny rural town of Rowley, the clerk demonstrated just one of many big-hearted gestures, opening for business at 5 a.m. to allow a town selectman and his partner to file for a license.

The vast majority of couples who applied for marriage licenses on May 17 returned to their local city and town halls to pick up their licenses on May 20. Boston's Arlington Street Church, a Unitarian landmark, acknowledged the importance of the day by throwing open its doors at 8:30 a.m. for nonstop weddings. In one of the first ceremonies of the day, the church's minister, the Reverend Kim Crawford Harvie, and her partner were married by Rabbi Howard Berman. Crawford Harvie then reciprocated for Rabbi Berman and his partner. Then Berman, Crawford Harvie, and the Reverend George Whitehouse married forty-nine couples, concluding with a 9 p.m. ceremony scheduled for a church member.

Every twenty minutes a new couple, sometimes with just each other, other times with children and even pets, walked down the aisle to say their vows. Each ceremony began with the acknowledgment that the couple had been "married in their hearts" for years, and that the wedding represented "the official recognition of the Commonwealth of Massachusetts." For Paul O'Brien and David Nielson of Quincy, a couple for eighteen years, that was certainly true. They had always seen themselves as married, but they wanted the legal protections of marriage, especially to make decisions around health care for each other. O'Brien spoke of his relief from one of the fears on the minds of many same-sex couples: "Family can't come in and ever take us away from one another."

Across the river at Cambridge City Hall, the line was out the door for a good part of the day. Cheers and tears wove a web around the waiting families. Couples watched as others married throughout the now even-more historic building and out on the lawn. In the bright sunlight, Jennifer Hess, a Massachusetts Freedom to Marry Coalition board member, her partner, Jennifer Bragdon, and their two children, Emmett, eleven, and Cinta Anyka, twenty, became a legal family. Hess, who had lived overseas for much of her life, later reflected on her emotions at the time. "I felt that my feet had firmly landed in this great country, on this rich, free soil. I felt that I finally stood shoulder-to-shoulder with my fellow Americans because I had become entitled to participate in a civil marriage with the person I love."

Facing page
GLAD celebrates the beginning of same-sex marriage with a victory party at the Colonnade Hotel. *Goodridge* plaintiff Dave Wilson, a grandfather himself, and Annie Goodridge dance the night away.

This page
Carole and Nancy Allen Scannell marry in a large spring wedding at Apsley Mansion in Hudson, with family and friends there to share their love and joy.

Facing page
Among the families celebrating at Arlington Street Church were M. J. Knoll, Christine Finn, and their four-year-old son, Henry. After the wedding, Henry concluded on his own, "Now we're all Knoll-Finns."

Donald Twomey and Michael Davison were
married by Rabbi Howard Berman at the Arlington
Street Church. Their sons, Seth and Luke, participated in the ceremony.

Jennifer Bragdon, Emmett Bragdon-Hess,
Jennifer Hess, and Zap pose in their kitchen. A
couple for nineteen years, the women also have
a twenty-year-old daughter, Cinta Anyka.

The best part of being married is that now when we walk down the street, people won't just see two guys and a kid, they'll have to see a FAMILY.

—*Sasha, thirteen-year-old son of John McDargh and Tim Dunn*

BUT ALL WAS NOT JOY AND JUSTICE

The celebratory atmosphere of the spring weddings was marred by the insistence of the governor that same-sex marriages of out-of-state couples would be null and void. Seeking a wider stage for his conservative views, Governor Romney resurrected the state's moribund 1913 law requiring a couple's home state to recognize the marriage in order for it to be legal. Mary Bonauto pointed out that the 1913 law, originally used to prevent out-of-state interracial couples from marrying in Massachusetts, "was given birth for discriminatory purposes and is being revived for discriminatory purposes." Unfazed, Romney contacted the attorney general in every state and warned them that their gay and lesbian citizens might try to marry in Massachusetts. Arline Isaacson quipped, "Someone should tell him he's the governor of Massachusetts, not of the United States."

Despite the threats, out-of-state couples, filled with optimism, made their way to the commonwealth just as three months earlier others had flocked to San Francisco when Mayor Gavin Newsom had announced the city would marry same-sex couples. From as far away as Florida, Maryland, and California and as near as Vermont, a state with civil unions, they came to Massachusetts to publicly declare their love—and, hopefully, legally sanction their unions.

Though the governor was determined to stop their marriages, out-of-state couples had allies among city officials. In urban Somerville, the mayor greeted couples on the steps of City Hall with the words, "If you're from out of state, welcome to Somerville." In a number of other municipalities, among them Springfield, Northampton, Worcester, Attleboro, and the gay mecca of Provincetown, at the tip of Cape Cod, city clerks also married whoever crossed the threshold.

In a rare act of defiance, thirteen town clerks later sued the state for demanding that they selectively enforce the 1913 law. The governor and attorney general directed the clerks to refuse licenses to all nonresident same-sex couples rather than offering them the same form that nonresidents heterosexual couples were asked to sign, verifying that they knew of no impediment to their marriage in their home states. ACLU of Massachusetts attorney Sarah Wunsch lauded the clerks, noting that they "deserved enormous respect for challenging directives from the attorney general and the governor that ordered them to discriminate and violate their oath to uphold the constitution of Massachusetts." On behalf of the clerks, the ACLU argued that "the state's resurrection of a moribund 1913 law, simply for the purpose of discriminating against gay and lesbian couples who came to Massachusetts to marry, was impermissible." Unfortunately, the SJC disagreed, and in April 2006 the clerks lost their final appeal, as did five of the seven out-of-state couples who attempted to overturn the state's decision to void their marriages. Couples from New York and Rhode Island, whose states did not explicitly ban same-sex marriage, were allowed to return to the trial court to sue for the right to marry in Massachusetts; however, the New York case was unable to proceed when, a few months later, New York's high court ruled that same-sex couples did not have the right to marry there. On September 29, the Rhode Island plaintiffs won their case, but for the vast majority of lesbians and gay men to marry in Massachusetts, the 1913 law will have to be repealed.

DEFENSE OF MARRIAGE ACTS
HURT FAMILIES—PURPOSEFULLY

The ease with which Governor Romney was able to resurrect the 1913 law banning out-of-state couples from marrying in Massachusetts was in part the result of federal and state Defense of Marriage Acts passed between 1996 and 2004. These DOMAs allow states to refuse to recognize same-sex marriages performed in other states. For gay and lesbian couples this puts severe limitations on their marriages. Not only are out-of-state couples unable to come to Massachusetts to marry, but married Massachusetts same-sex couples cannot count on their marriages being recognized if they travel or move to another state. In addition, the federal government denies same-sex couples and their families the security of more than one thousand federal benefits that come with a marriage license.

Marcia Kadish and Tanya McCloskey, the first couple to marry on May 17, realized this in 2006, when Marcia had a car accident in Connecticut. As Tanya frantically called the state police in Connecticut, she remembered to identify Marcia as her sister, not her spouse. In Connecticut, Marcia and Tanya's marriage would be meaningless, and mentioning it might undermine their safety even further. Ironically, if the accident had happened in Canada, their marriage would have been honored, with access and information granted immediately.

The purposefully discriminatory aspects of the federal DOMA are most hurtful to married seniors in the lesbian and gay community. Without access to the federal benefits that come with a marriage license—for example, Social Security survivor benefits, tax and inheritance benefits, and joint property ownership—they face growing old with little of the financial security that married heterosexuals take for granted.

When Marion Kenneally, seventy-one, talks of her marriage to her partner of twenty-six years, Anna Bissonette, seventy-three, she smiles broadly. "We already felt married to each other physically, romantically, and spiritually. What we gained under the law were some of the same rights and protections enjoyed by our straight relatives and friends who are married." Marion adds, "Having our large extended families and friends at our wedding was important to us. Our marriage gives us validation as a couple."

Both of these well-loved and fiercely independent women have given much of their lives in service to others—Anna as a nurse and advocate protecting seniors from homelessness and Marion as a public school teacher. Now, in Massachusetts, as a married couple they have the right to take care of each other. But as they age, they worry about finances and protecting their home without the inheritance, Social Security, and tax benefits that the federal government grants heterosexual married couples. Marion nonetheless thinks positively about the struggle for marriage equality: "I dream of the day when all lesbian and gay people will be able to marry—not just in Massachusetts, but in all states and all over the world—and receive the benefits they need and deserve."

Don Picard and Robert DeBenedictis sit with their children, Carmen, six, and James, two. Robert and Don committed to love and care for each other at their wedding on October 11, 1997. On May 17, 2004, they completed the paperwork to make their wedding legal in the eyes of the state.

Randy Quinones Akee and KJ Ward pose with Shaka. Following a favorable court ruling in 1993, Randy, a Native Hawaiian, and his partner, KJ, hoped that Hawaii would be the first state to legalize marriage for same-sex couples. While studying and working in Massachusetts, they were able to realize their dream of marrying. In Germany, where they now live, their marriage is fully recognized.

Michelle Coleman and Pamela Waterman,
together for six years, married October 10, 2004.

*W*hen we leave this church, there are forces of anger, ignorance, and hate that seek to tear asunder the bonds of this marriage. . . . All over this country, for many years to come, the battle will rage. But . . . the inexorable march toward full equality cannot be stopped.

—*Representative Mike Festa, at the wedding of*
Senator Jarrett Barrios and Doug Hattaway

PROCLAIMING OUR LOVE AND PROTECTING OUR FAMILIES

Despite the limitations, Massachusetts same-sex couples are marrying to publicly declare their love and commitment to one another and to protect their families as fully as possible. At home in Massachusetts, thousands of same-sex couples have found a new level of acceptance as well as the added security of knowing that having a marriage license can make a difference.

Dawn and Marilyn

Dawn Paul realized what a difference a legal marriage made just a few weeks after she married her partner of twenty-seven years, Marilyn McCrory. The couple was out kayaking when Marilyn became ill and was taken by ambulance to the hospital. Says Dawn, "In that time of fear and confusion, it was good to be able to tell members of the hospital's staff that we were married—no long explanations, no worries about our legal status, no justifications about why I should be allowed to make decisions or ask questions about Marilyn's care—just to say when asked, 'We're married.'" Being recognized as next of kin, particularly in times of medical emergencies, is one of the most significant tangible benefits that marriage offers Massachusetts same-sex couples.

Steve and Bill

Steve Galante and his partner, Bill Pluckhahn, met, fell in love, and, in more than thirteen years together, adopted five children. Deeply engaged with their community, they feel genuinely loved by neighbors and friends, who are often floored by their commitment to raise five children with special needs.

Constantly seeking to protect their family, they committed to each other in a church ceremony in 1993 and traveled to Vermont for a civil union in 2001. In 2004, they married in a large wedding with their parents, siblings, and friends gathered in celebration of them and their five children. Ben, the oldest, sang, "You Raise Me Up," and there wasn't a dry eye in the chapel. Steve realized their wedding was different from their previous commitment

Facing page
Bill Pluckhahn and Steve Galante with their children, Ben, Zach, Amanda, Mary Grace, and Deon.

ceremonies: "Having a legal marriage, I think, made it 'okay' for anyone who doubted themselves for wanting to be supportive and accepting of our family. When marriage was made legal, it relieved people of their moral struggle with this particular issue. It allowed them to follow their hearts, their best instincts, and embrace our family."

Bill adds that the "affirmation and pride that our children felt on that day with all of the significant adults and children in our lives present was important. The kids knew that our family was every bit as valid and legal and worthy as all the other families they knew."

Julie and Olga

For Julie Whitlow and Olga Merchan, the struggle to keep their family together has been long and arduous. Olga is an immigrant from Colombia, and she and Julie fell in love back in the early 1990s. In 1999, they adopted their first child, Marina, an infant from Guatemala. Her sister, Mattea, came a few years later.

If heterosexual immigrants marry U.S. citizens, their spouses may sponsor them for citizenship, but Julie and Olga did not have this option. For years, Olga worked at getting permanent residency status so she could remain with her partner and adopted children in the United States. The psychological and financial toll on the couple and their family, however, was enormous. It cost upward of $15,000 in legal fees for Olga to obtain a permanent-residency green card.

Even with permanent residency granted and recorded on the federal computer system, threats to their family continued. Returning from nine months in Nicaragua, where Julie had been teaching as a Fulbright scholar, the family, struggling with suitcases, diaper bags, snacks, and children, were separated by customs authorities. Olga, still awaiting her official identification card, was sent to another area in customs by a chuckling official who said, "The United States does not recognize *that* kind of family." Julie worried that "a petty border guard with a streak of homophobia had the power to take Olga away and potentially find an excuse to detain her." The family knew full well that a married heterosexual couple with young children would never face that kind of trauma reentering the country.

Back in Massachusetts for just over a month in the summer of 2004, Julie and Olga took the next step to protect their family. With Marina as bridesmaid and Mattea in Julie's arms, they married in their garden, with friends and family members present to witness the historic occasion. Weeks later, the first symbol of equity, a letter from the commonwealth acknowledging that Olga was now insured under Julie's family health plan, won a prominent place on the refrigerator. Because of the federal Defense of Marriage Act, Julie still couldn't sponsor Olga for citizenship, but after a ten-year struggle, in 2006 the official green card finally arrived. Olga now has it in hand to show to any border guard.

*H*as our life changed since the day we were married? Unequivocally, yes. From the smallest of incidents, such as filling out an application and being legitimately able to say I am married, to the bigger events—for example, when I was in the emergency room at Beth Israel and they asked if there was anyone in the waiting room they should bring in, I said, "My husband," and no one batted an eye; they just brought Bruce back to my room.

—*George Smart*

Olga Merchan and Julie Whitlow with their
children, Marina and Mattea.

*W*hen I looked in the eyes of the children living with these couples, I decided that I don't feel at this time that same-sex marriage has hurt the commonwealth in any way. In fact I would say that in my view it has had a good effect for the children in these families.

—*Senator James Timilty (who ran for office as an opponent of same-sex marriage)*

The Unitarian Universalist Association celebrated the first anniversary of the *Goodridge* decision with a party at their Beacon Street headquarters, where a year earlier the Reverend William Sinkford had married Julie and Hillary Goodridge. Here, the plaintiffs and their attorney, surprised by an explosion of confetti, prepare to cut the anniversary cake. (L-R: Gary Chalmers, Maureen Brodoff, Ellen Wade, Rob Compton, Dave Wilson, Gloria Bailey, Linda Davies, Mary Bonauto, Julie and Hillary Goodridge)

*I*t's wonderful that we've been able to marry, but unlike heterosexual couples, we have to worry that this right that is so precious and that we struggled so hard to obtain could be taken away.

—Goodridge *plaintiff Ellen Wade*

Molly Butterworth and Davida Wegner celebrate
the one-year anniversary of marriage equality at
Cambridge City Hall.

Lawrence Chien, Joe Yau, and Jay Wang mark the one-year anniversary of the *Goodridge* ruling at a GLAD party.

A LOVE WORTHY OF RESPECT

On May 17, 2005, Tom Lang and Alex Westerhoff celebrated their first wedding anniversary by standing all day in front of the State House with a four-foot-by-eight-foot handmade sign that read, THANK YOU, MASSACHUSETTS, FOR 1 YEAR OF EQUALITY. On the same day former chief executive of Bank of America, Chad Gifford, and his wife, Anne, noted the marriage equality anniversary in the op-ed pages of the *Boston Globe*. "After seven years in a committed relationship, our son and his partner exchanged vows in front of 125 friends and family members. It brought home the reality that marriage is about two people who love each other and who desire to commit to a life together." After a year of same-sex marriage, growing numbers in Massachusetts had come to understand that same-sex marriage is about the same thing as heterosexual marriage—whom we choose to love and whom we call family.

For the children of same-sex couples, having their families legitimized has been particularly important. As Julian Baptista explained in a paean for his moms, "On this Mother's Day—nearly two years after the state allowed same-sex couples to be legally married—I feel lucky to have two cards to deliver. More than anything I am thankful that my friends now see that my family is just as valued and important as their family is." Julian's friends now know that the love between people of the same sex is as worthy of respect as that of heterosexuals.

Eighteen months after the *Goodridge* decision and the marriages of thousands of same-sex couples in Massachusetts, David O'Brien, Loyola Professor of Roman Catholic Studies at the Jesuit College of the Holy Cross, reflected on the importance of love in religious teachings and in our lives. In the *Boston Globe*, he posed questions and answers reminiscent of the old Baltimore Catechism, a well-known fixture of Catholic training, asking, "Where do we find God? In love for one another, and that includes the day-to-day decision to love this person with whom one lives." O'Brien went on, "What happened in those towers and those captured planes on 9/11? Hundreds of people called people they loved to speak at the end of love." O'Brien suggested to his readers that the next time someone starts an argument about gay marriage, they pose the question, "Does love matter, or doesn't it?"

Love does matter. So does marriage.

Marriage means nothing and everything to us. It means nothing, in a sense, because we were fully a family before the ceremony, with fifteen years and two kids and a vision of our future together, and we did not need a legal certificate or a ceremony to validate that. And yet, and yet . . . we are now, in fact, legal. Legally married in the eyes of the church and in the eyes of the commonwealth.

—Judy Hudson

Kathy Humphrey and Judy Hudson married in a September 2004 wedding at Eliot Church in Newton. Their daughter, Sasha, was a little anxious about walking down the aisle, so Judy reassured her that she could walk with her brother, Jake.

Kathy Humphrey and Judy Hudson say their vows.

Marianne Stravinskas, Liz Page, and their daughter, Chloe

*A*t school, Chloe was speaking to her teacher, who was wearing a wedding ring. She asked him if he was married and he replied "yes." Chloe then asked him innocently, "to a girl or to a boy?" We love this story because it illustrates her natural acceptance of love between any two people.

—Liz Page

ACKNOWLEDGMENTS

Many people have been generous in helping us work on assembling this history of the struggle for marriage equality in Massachusetts. We want to thank the American Civil Liberties Union of Massachusetts, Karen Rudolph and Jimi Simmons, and Wainwright Bank for providing financial support without which the project could never have been completed. We thank Elyse Cherry of Boston Community Capital for shepherding this project to reality.

Mary Bonauto, Evelyn C. White, and Hillary Goodridge provided the inspiration to get Marilyn Humphries to believe that her remarkable photographic history of the marriage equality movement should be preserved in a book. We agreed with them and volunteered to do the research and writing, capturing a great deal of the history that we ourselves have lived through as activists, historians, and writers.

We are especially grateful to all the people who shared their stories of these extraordinary past few years. In particular, we want to thank Mary Bonauto, Arline Isaacson, Norma Shapiro, Marty Rouse, and Marc Solomon for giving us their perspectives on the political dimensions of the story. This book would not have been possible without the dedication of the members of the Massachusetts Gay and Lesbian Political Caucus, Gay & Lesbian Advocates & Defenders, the American Civil Liberties Union of Massachusetts, the Freedom to Marry Coalition, and MassEquality, all of whom worked tirelessly for marriage equality.

The *Goodridge* plaintiff couples have given generously of their time throughout the period of the court case and the political struggle that followed. We thank them for the many interviews they gave to the press and to us, and for graciously allowing their photographs to be taken. We also thank the many same-sex couples who have shared their stories of marriage over the last two years.

We appreciate the careful reading that so many of our friends and colleagues gave to various drafts of the text: Chris Cornog, Peg Elson, Vicky Fortino, Steve Galante, Beth Hogan, Kate Hogan, Jim Jackson, Susan Johnson, Janie King, Helen Lewis, Lynn Nadeau, Pat Ould, Bill Pluckhahn, Sue Sherry, Karen Rudolph, and Barbara Taylor.

For technical and research assistance, we thank The History Project: Documenting LGBT Boston, Andrea Still, Libby Bouvier, Luis Aponte-Pares, Bruce Bell, Sarah Wunsch, Marjorie Kelly, Scott Edelstein, the Kalenakai Gang of Kaneohe, and Fleur Stewart.

For their continued support in large and small ways throughout the past year, thank you to Olga Merchan and Julie Whitlow, Dick Elia, Cathy Burack, Kathy Pratt and Alicia Curtis, and the very patient staff of the Paraprofessional Healthcare Institute. Our families have been supportive in important ways, and for that we are very grateful.

Finally, we wish to thank Beacon Press, particularly Helene Atwan, Brian Halley, and P.J. Tierney, for their faith in this project and their support in turning our vision into a reality.

A NOTE ON THE SOURCES

The reconstruction of events in *Courting Equality* relies heavily on newspaper accounts of the marriage equality struggle. In particular, we are grateful for the terrific reporting in the *Boston Globe, Boston Herald, Springfield Republican*, and the *Worcester Telegram & Gazette. Bay Windows* deserves a special mention for being an important voice of the lesbian, gay, bisexual, and transgender community. Reporters Laura Kiritsy and Ethan Jacobs offered poignant stories about our community that often appeared with Marilyn Humphries's photographs. In addition, we participated in many of the historic events recounted here, going back to the 1970s, and we have relied on our own experiences, which have included demonstrating and lobbying for the gay and lesbian civil rights bill, challenging the state's foster-care policy, bringing attention to the AIDS crisis, marching on Washington, and supporting marriage equality.

The pathbreaking court cases throughout New England that are playing a central role in achieving marriage equality are documented on the Gay & Lesbian Advocates & Defenders Web site. The Web site was an invaluable resource for us. The central role that the Massachusetts legislature played in shaping the discourse around marriage equality is documented in unedited video of the constitutional convention sessions recorded by WGBH's *Gavel to Gavel*. These video recordings and tapes are available at the State Library of

Massachusetts, Special Collections. Unless otherwise noted, remarks from the legislators throughout the book are all from this collection.

For understanding the context in which this story unfolded, we are indebted to two excellent sources: George Chauncey's *Why Marriage? The History Shaping Today's Debate over Gay Equality* (Basic Books, 2004) and Evan Wolfson's *Why Marriage Matters: America, Equality, and Gay People's Right to Marry* (Simon & Schuster, 2004).

NOTES

INTRODUCTION

"It is impossible":

Mary Bonauto, *"Goodridge* in Context," *Harvard Civil Rights–Civil Liberties Law Review* 40, no. 1 (Winter 2005): 5.

"searing for me":

Except where otherwise noted, quotes from Mary Bonauto are from her interview with the authors, tape recording, Portland, ME, May 19, 2006. Some facts are also drawn from David Garrow, "Toward a More Perfect Union," *New York Times Magazine*, May 9, 2004.

As GLAD explained:

Mary Bonauto et al. Brief of plaintiffs-appellants in *Goodridge v. Department of Public Health*, 798 N.E. 2d 941 (Mass. 2003); 2-7. Available at www.glad.org/marriage/Goodridge/Appellants_Brief.pdf.

The state argued:

Thomas Reilly et al. Brief of defendants-appellees, *Goodridge v. Department of Public Health* 798 N.E. 2d 941 (Mass. 2003), available at www.glad.org/marriage/Goodridge/Appellees_Brief.pdf.

In the United States, nearly 40 percent of marriages:

Evan Wolfson, *Why Marriage Matters: America, Equality, and Gay People's Right to Marry* (New York: Simon & Schuster, 2004), 111.

Recognizing the desire:

MCC's history is discussed in George Chauncey, *Why Marriage? The History Shaping Today's Debate over Gay Equality* (New York: Basic Books, 2004).

On May 18, 1970:

Baker and McConnell's story is documented in Dudley Clendinen and Adam Nagourney, *Out for Good* (New York: Simon & Schuster, 1999).

"result in an undermining":

ibid., 56–57.

Media headlines decried:

Peggy Pascoe, "Sex, Gender, and Same-Sex Marriage," in *Is Academic Feminism Dead?*, eds. Social Justice Group at the Center for Advanced Feminist Studies, University of Minnesota (New York: New York University Press, 2000), 92–93.

Nationally, anti-gay sentiment peaked:

Chauncey, *Why Marriage?* All polling data from pages 48–55.

Evan Wolfson, co-counsel:

ibid., 125.

In 1995, local activists:

For a thorough discussion of the Vermont case, see David Moats, *Civil Wars: The Battle for Gay Marriage* (New York: Harcourt, 2004).

"I felt like our": Mary Bonauto quoted in

Chauncey, *Why Marriage?*, 127–128.

"personal decisions relating":

Lawrence v. Texas, referring to
previous U.S. Supreme Court decisions
in *Griswold v. Connecticut* 381 U. S. 479
(1965), in which the Court affirmed the
right of married couples to choose to
use birth control; *Roe v. Wade* 410 U. S.
113 (1973), legalizing abortion; and
*Planned Parenthood of Southeastern
Pennsylvania v. Casey* 505 U. S. 833,
850 (1992), reaffirming the *Roe v.
Wade* decision.

"a vocabulary in":

Evan Wolfson quoted in Chauncey,
Why Marriage?, 125.

50 percent supported:

Frank Phillips and Rick Klein, "50 %
in Poll Back SJC Ruling," *Boston Globe*,
November 21, 2003.

"Massachusetts is our":

Lou Sheldon quoted in Thomas
Caywood, "Right Wing Revs Up for
'Last Stand' in Bay State," *Boston
Herald*, November 21, 2003.

CALL-OUTS

"It was in Massachusetts":

Evan Wolfson, *Why Marriage*

Matters, 186.

CHAPTER 1: DIGNITY AND EQUALITY
FOR ALL: THE GOODRIDGE DECISION

"The Court declared":

Mary Bonauto, quoted in George
Chauncey, *Why Marriage? The History
Shaping Today's Debate over Gay
Equality* (New York: Basic Books,
2004), 135.

GLAD legal team and its allies:

GLAD's major allies in the same-sex
marriage court case and ensuing legislative battles included the American
Civil Liberties Union (ACLU) of
Massachusetts, the Massachusetts
Gay and Lesbian Political Caucus
(MGLPC), and MassEquality,
itself a coalition of more than
sixty organizations.

Gina and Heidi:

Gina Nortonsmith and Heidi
Nortonsmith, interview by authors,
Northampton, MA, November 5, 2005.

Gary and Rich:

Gary Chalmers and Rich Linnell,
interview by authors, Whitinsville,
MA, November 12, 2005.

Gloria and Linda: Gloria Bailey and Linda
Davies, interview by authors, Orleans,
MA, October 31, 2005.

Ellen and Maureen:

Ellen Wade and Maureen Brodoff,
interview by authors, Newton, MA,
November 12, 2005.

Hillary and Julie:

Hillary and Julie Goodridge, interview
by Danielle Schulman, tape recording,
Jamaica Plain, MA, April 21, 2004.

"I think I was":

Mike Horgan and Ed Balmelli
quoted in Laura Kiritsy, "Victory
in Massachusetts," *Bay Windows*,
November 18, 2003.

Dave and Rob:

David Wilson and Rob Compton,
interview by Danielle Schulman,
tape recording, Jamaica Plain, MA,
April 26, 2004.

"Wow, this is":

Mary Bonauto quoted in Laura
Kiritsy, "Court Rules Couples May
Wed," *Bay Windows*, November
18, 2003.

"A court finally":

Mary Bonauto quoted in Kathleen
Burge, "Gays Have Right to Marry,

SJC Says in Historic Ruling—Legislature Given 180 Days to Change Law," *Boston Globe*, November 19, 2003.

"The issue in":
Mary Bonauto quoted in Laura Kiritsy, "Victory in Massachusetts," *Bay Windows*, November 18, 2003.

"We are a couple":
Julie Goodridge quoted in Laura Kiritsy, "Court Rules Couples May Wed," *Bay Windows*, November 18, 2003.

"My partner of":
Gary Chalmers quoted in Shaun Sutner, "SJC Clears Way for Gay Marriage—Mass. Legislature Must Change Laws," *Worcester Telegram & Gazette*, November 19, 2003.

"It means I'm":
David Wilson and Gina Smith quoted in Anonymous, "Landmark Ruling: The Victors," *Boston Herald*, November 19, 2003.

"I agree with":
Governor Mitt Romney quoted in Frank Phillips and Rick Klein, "Lawmakers Are Divided on Response," *Boston Globe*, November 19, 2003.

"Such a profound":
Attorney General Thomas Reilly quoted in Kathleen Burge, "Gays Have Right to Marry, SJC Says in Historic Ruling—Legislature Given 180 Days to Change Law," *Boston Globe*, November 19, 2003.

"I kept thinking":
Arline Isaacson quoted in Jennifer Peter, "Reilly's Stance Upsets Gays," *The Republican*, November 22, 2003.

"I am mindful":
President George W. Bush quoted in Derrick Jackson, "Mass Court Cuts through Homophobia," *Boston Globe*, November 19, 2003.

"Marriage is a":
President George W. Bush quoted in Anne Kornblut, "Some Republicans See Decision as a Stance to Run against in '04," *Boston Globe*, November 19, 2003.

"Homosexual behavior":
Evelyn T. Reilly quoted in Dan Ring, "Court Backs Gay Marriage, Declares State Ban Is Illegal," *The Republican*, November 19, 2003.

"This is truly":
Laurie A. Letourneau and Sean O'Malley quoted in Kathleen A. Shaw,

"Religious Leaders Take Sides—Bishop 'Dismayed, Disappointed,'" *Worcester Telegram & Gazette*, November 19, 2003.

"a welcome milestone":
Senator Edward Kennedy quoted in David R. Guarino and Andrew Miga, "Landmark Ruling: Dem Candidates Embrace Spirit but Keep Distance," *Boston Herald*, November 19, 2003.

"impose its will":
John F. Kennedy quoted in Evan Wolfson, *Why Marriage Matters: America, Equality, and Gay People's Right to Marry* (New York: Simon & Schuster, 2004), 103.

"We have witnessed":
Rev. Nancy Taylor and Rev. William G. Sinkford quoted in Michael Paulson, "Strong, Divided Opinions Mark Clergy Response," *Boston Globe*, November 19, 2003.

"extremely gutsy":
Lawrence Tribe quoted in Jules Crittenden, "Landmark Ruling: 'Legal Chaos' Decision May Spark Lawsuits across the Nation," *Boston Herald*, November 19, 2003.

"I actually feel":
Scott Gortikov and Bridget Snell

quoted in Yvonne Abraham, "Among Same-Sex Couples, Proposals, Tears Flow," *Boston Globe*, November 19, 2003.

"If marriage licenses":
Mary Bonauto quoted in Elizabeth J. Beardsley, "Gays Rip Pols on Union Bill," *Boston Herald*, November 22, 2003.

"They think that":
Marianne Duddy quoted in Eric Convey, "Church Vows to Fight Gay Marriage, Catholics Pressure Pols," *Boston Herald*, November 29, 2003.

"I continue to":
Sen. Jarrett Barrios quoted in Laura Kiritsy, "Civil Unions: Swimming against the Tide? Legislators to File Civil Unions Bills in Response to *Goodridge* Ruling," *Bay Windows*, December 11, 2003.

"There is no":
Scott Harshbarger et al. quoted in Laura Kiritsy, "Weld Leads Group Urging Legislature on Marriage, Letters [sic] Tells Lawmakers to Enact *Goodridge*," *Bay Windows*, January 8, 2004.

On the following:
For a full listing of the more than sixty groups that are part of this coalition see www.massequality.org/pdfs/coalitionmembers.pdf.

"I come from":
Gary Daffin quoted in Ethan Jacobs, "Pro Same-Sex Marriage Rally Packs Statehouse; Gathering Calls for Enactment of *Goodridge*, Rejection of Constitutional Amendment," *Bay Windows*, January 15, 2004.

"It's about judicial":
Laurie A. Letourneau quoted in Laura Kiritsy, "Same-Sex Marriage Opponents to Host Rallies across Mass., Gatherings Planned for Worcester, Fall River and Springfield," *Bay Windows*, January 22, 2004.

"They are dressing":
Arline Isaacson quoted in Raphael Lewis, "Gay Marriage Foes Push Amendment—Coalition Formed to Fight SJC Ruling," *Boston Globe*, January 8, 2004.

"Today any confusion":
Mary Bonauto quoted in Laura Kiritsy, "SJC: Civil Unions Don't Cut It," *Bay Windows*, February 5, 2004.

"We've heard from":
Governor Mitt Romney quoted in Shaun Sutner, "SJC Rules Gays Entitled to Marry—Court Clears the Way for Same-Sex Nuptials," *Worcester Telegram & Gazette*, February 5, 2004.

"I think and":
Gary Chalmers quoted in ibid.

"I'm glad the":
Gina Smith quoted in Dan Ring, "Court Backs Gay Marriage," *The Republican*, February 5, 2004.

CALL-OUTS

"The SJC ruling offers a vision":
Boston Globe editors, "Equal Rights—and Rites," *Boston Globe*, November 19, 2003.

"If the KKK":
Quoted in Frank Phillips and Raphael Lewis, "A Hunt for Middle Ground—Travaglini Voices Confidence on a Marriage Accord Today," *Boston Globe*, March 11, 2004.

CHAPTER 2: EARLY MILESTONES:
THE STRUGGLE FOR FAMILY EQUALITY

The 1972 gay pride march:
This account of events is from Dudley Clendinen and Adam Nagourney,

Out for Good (New York: Simon & Schuster, 1999), 127.

Two organizations emerged:

All the gay and lesbian organizations that have contributed to the civil rights struggle over the years are too numerous to name. Several that have been particularly important to establishing family equality include the Massachusetts Gay and Lesbian Bar Association, Fenway Community Health Center, and the Freedom to Marry Coalition.

Why Marriage?:

The analysis presented here owes much to George Chauncey's excellent book *Why Marriage? The History Shaping Today's Debate over Gay Marriage* (New York: Basic Books, 2004).

Lesbian and Gay Parents Project:

This discussion of the Lesbian and Gay Parents Project is based on Gail Shister, "Gay Parents Fight for Legal Equality," *Boston Globe*, February 8, 1979.

legal issues became more salient:

In the 1980s, gay fathers were still relatively rare. Parenting among men became much more common in the 1990s.

Foster Equality:

The version of events discussed here is taken primarily from Laura Benkov, *Reinventing the Family* (New York: Crown Publishers, 1994), 86–98.

"We wish to make it clear":

Donald Babets and David Jean quoted in Chris Black, "Gay Couple Challenges State's Removal of Foster Children," *Boston Globe*, May 11, 1985.

"The goal of foster care":

Boston Globe editors, "A Normal Home Setting," *Boston Globe*, May 13, 1985.

"a homosexual or bisexual orientation":

Laura Briggs, "Mass. House Votes to Ban Gay Foster Parents," *Gay Community News*, May 27, 1990.

"I am thrilled":

Laura Briggs, "Mass. to End Gay Foster Parent Ban," *Gay Community News*, April 8,1990.

"The one who just":

Arline Isaacson quoted in "Domestic Partners," State House News Service, JT, April 27, 1994, available at www.mglpc.org/story.php?id=11.

With domestic partnership:

The more progressive Massachusetts senate voted in favor of domestic partnership in several legislative sessions beginning in 1998.

The second-parent adoption case:

In *Adoption of Tammy* 619 N.E.2d. 315 (Mass.1993), the SJC ruled that Dr. Helen Cooksey could adopt the biological daughter of her partner, nationally known breast cancer specialist Dr. Susan Love. *Adoption of Tammy* was decided in tandem with *Adoption of Susan* in which Ellen Wade sought to adopt the biological daughter of her partner, Maureen Brodoff. Wade and Brodoff later became plaintiffs in the *Goodridge* case. In the adoption case, they were also represented by GLAD attorney Mary Bonauto.

"would be recognized":

Jack Meyers, "We Are Families," *Boston Herald*, September 12, 1993.

thousand-plus federal benefits:

Notably, married gay and lesbian couples in Massachusetts are still excluded from these federal benefits as a result of the federal Defense of Marriage Act passed in 1996.

"the fiercest battle over gay rights":

Stephanie Ebbert, "Battle over Gay Marriage Petition Gets Ugly," *Boston Globe*, November 21, 2001.

"a thundercloud of boos":
All quotes by Sen. Thomas Birmingham from Scott A. Giordano, "Person of the Year: Tom Birmingham," *Bay Windows*, December 27, 2002.

"Call me old-fashioned":
Gubernatorial candidate Mitt Romney quoted in Laura Kiritsy, "Election 2002: Don't Dismiss Romney, Gay Republicans Say," *Bay Windows*, October 24, 2002. Romney used this line during an October 2002 gubernatorial election debate.

"an attack on the common good":
Sean O'Malley quoted in Yvonne Abraham, "O'Malley Calls Gay Marriage a Threat—Archbishop Opposes Definition Change," *Boston Globe*, October 3, 2003. In the spring of 2003, polls already showed 50 percent of Massachusetts residents supporting same-sex marriage. See Frank Phillips, "Support for Gay Marriage: Mass. Poll Finds Half in Favor," *Boston Globe*, April 8, 2003.

CALL-OUTS

"The administration is exploiting people's worst fears":
Quoted in Chris Black, "Policy Praised by Legislators, Protest by Gay Community," *Boston Globe*, May 25, 1985.

"This is a civil rights bill":
Quoted in "Sexual Discrimination," State House News Service, May 5, 1987.

"The first line of protection":
Quoted in Linda Wheeler, "Mass Wedding Marries Tradition and Protest," *Washington Post*, April 25, 1993.

"We have been expecting the Christian Coalition":
Quoted in Peter Cassels, "Cambridge's Domestic Partners Plan Is Challenged in Court," *Bay Windows*, March 23, 2000.

"There are some issues where I feel strongly":
Quoted in Scott Giordano, "Person of the Year: Tom Birmingham," *Bay Windows*, December 27, 2002.

CHAPTER 3: SEPARATE BUT EQUAL?: DEFENDING MARRIAGE EQUALITY

"A constitutional amendment":
Coretta Scott King speaking at the Richard Stockton College of New Jersey. Quoted in Associated Press, "Coretta Scott King Gives Her Support to Marriage Equality," March 24, 2004, available at www.massequality.org/supporters/allies_supp/2004_king.html.

The budget for:
Sean Cahill, *Same-Sex Marriage in the United States: Focus on the Facts* (Lanham, MD: Lexington Books, 2004), 21.

"Initially, thinking of two men":
Steven Tolman quoted in Raphael Lewis, "Facing a Difficult Decision," *Boston Globe*, February 8, 2004.

The pro-equality lobby:
The professional lobbyists worked closely with a core group of leaders from MassEquality, GLAD, ACLU of Massachusetts, and the Freedom to Marry Coalition. These included MassEquality's campaign director Marty Rouse, political director Marc Solomon, communications consultant Mary Breslauer, and board member Holly Gunner; GLAD attorney Mary Bonauto; Freedom to Marry Coalition advocacy director Josh Friedes; and LGBT aging project director Amy Hunt.

Petersen shared his office:
Rep. Doug Petersen, remarks at The History Project: Documenting LGBT Boston exhibit, "From Boston

Marriage to Equal Marriage," May 14, 2005, Danvers, MA.

"make it easier for nongay":
Evan Wolfson quoted in George Chauncey, *Why Marriage? The History Shaping Today's Debate over Gay Marriage* (New York: Basic Books, 2004), 125.

67 percent of the membership:
Yvonne Abraham, "Church Sets Voter Drive to Fight Gay Marriage," *Boston Globe*, March 26, 2004.

"Civil unions are not equal":
Raphael Lewis and Yvonne Abraham, "Travaglini Hopeful of Compromise," *Boston Globe*, March 5, 2004.

Malia later reflected:
Liz Malia tells this story in Laura Kiritsy, "This Time It's Personal: Liz Malia," *Bay Windows*, April 8, 2004.

a shotgun marriage:
Ellen Goodman, "Strange Bedfellows on Gay Marriage," *Boston Globe*, April 1, 2004.

"faced a coordinated legal assault":
Mary L. Bonauto, "*Goodridge* in Context," *Harvard Civil Rights–Civil Liberties Law Review*, 40, No. 1 (2005): www.law.harvard.edu/students/orgs/crcl/vol40_1/bonauto.php. Bonauto's article carefully documents all of the cases that were filed by marriage equality opponents,

essentially the same people who had written briefs to support the Department of Public Health's denial of marriage licenses to the *Goodridge* plaintiffs. Among those who went to court to stop Massachusetts from issuing marriage licenses to same-sex couples were C. Joseph Doyle and Robert Largess of the Catholic Action League of Massachusetts; Pat Robertson's American Center for Law and Justice; former Vatican ambassador and Boston mayor Raymond Flynn; chairman of the Coalition to Preserve Traditional Marriage Thomas Shields; and thirteen state legislators who were same-sex marriage opponents. National conservative groups such as the Family Research Council, the Alliance Defense Fund, and the Law & Liberty Institute provided resources to the plaintiffs. In addition, Governor Romney sought a stay until the people were given a chance to vote on a constitutional amendment, a process that would have taken at least two and a half years.

Vowing retaliation at the ballot box:
Raphael Lewis and Michael Paulson, "Church Gives Pre-Election Scorecard—Gay Marriage Votes Identified in Mailings," *Boston Globe*, June 15, 2004.

the indictment on two charges:
Kevin Cullen, "Bishop Is Indicted but Won't Be Tried—Statute Limit Cited in Child Rape Case," *Boston Globe*, September 28, 2004. According to the article, "a Hampden County grand jury has indicted the Most. Rev. Thomas L. Dupre, the retired Roman Catholic bishop of Springfield, on two charges of child rape."

"Legislators would stick":
Marty Rouse, telephone conversation with P. Gozemba, tape recording, May 16, 2006.

"62 percent of Americans left":
Mary Bonauto and Marty Rouse, "Gay Marriage Is Not to Blame," *Boston Globe*, November 9, 2004.

"to create a new birth certificate":
Michael Levenson, "Birth Certificate Policy Draws Fire—Change Affects Same-Sex Couples," *Boston Globe*, July 22, 2005.

legislators were invited to the homes:
Marc Solomon, interview by authors, tape recording, Boston, MA, May 2, 2006.

"listening to find":
Norma Shapiro, interview by authors, tape recording, Boston, MA, May 2, 2006.

"what they jokingly referred to":

Laura Kiritsy, "Anatomy of a Victory," *Bay Windows*, September 22, 2005.

"[Goodridge] *as made stronger*": Petrucelli quoted in Laura Kiritsy, "East Boston Rep. Comes Out against Marriage Amendment," *Bay Windows*, August 18, 2005.

even though polls showed: A May 2005 poll, conducted by Decision Research for the MassEquality Education Fund, found that 62 percent of Massachusetts voters favored same-sex marriage.

A Pew Research Center: The Pew Research Center poll showed that between February 2004 and March 2006, the number of people "strongly opposed" to same-sex marriage dropped from 42 percent to 28 percent. http://people-press.org/reports/display.php3?ReportID=273.

CALL-OUTS

"For those legislators": Quoted in Jennifer Peter, "Statehouse Showdown," *Boston Globe*, February 11, 2004.

"Don't get me wrong": Quoted in "In Their Own Words," *Bay Windows*, March 18, 2004.

"The only God that I know":

Quoted in Ethan Jacobs, "Religious Leaders Weigh In on Marriage," *Bay Windows*, February 12, 2004.

"I didn't ever see": Quoted in Michael Paulson, "Walsh, St. Fleur Back Gay Marriage—State Lawmakers Firm in Faith, Belief," *Boston Globe*, February 11, 2005.

"Organized Catholicism is poised": Margery Egan, "Church Etiquette Takes Pass on Gays," *Boston Herald*, November 25, 2003.

"We want every legislator": Quoted in Laura Kiritsy, "Round Two," *Bay Windows*, March 11, 2004.

"The Supreme Judicial Court's decision": Devon Lerner, "Letter of Devon Lerner," *One Year of Marriage Equality* (Boston: MassEquality, 2005), 19.

"Today is a happy and proud day": Quoted in John J. Monahan, "Amendment Rejected—Same-Sex Vote Moot for Now," *Worcester Telegram & Gazette*, September 15, 2005.

CHAPTER 4: HERE COME THE BRIDES, HERE COME THE GROOMS: CELEBRATING MARRIAGE EQUALITY

"If people can do this": Marcia Hams quoted in Joanna Weiss and Anand Vaishnav, "Celebrations Envelop Cambridge City Hall," *Boston Globe*, May 17, 2004.

"It is a day to celebrate": Cambridge mayor Michael Sullivan quoted in Ethan Jacobs, "At Last!," *Bay Windows*, May 20, 2004.

"This is like winning": Susan Shepherd and Marcia Hams quoted in Yvonne Abraham and Rick Klein, "Free to Marry—Historic Day Arrives," *Boston Globe*, May 17, 2004.

"We got there": Paul McMahon quoted in Laura Kiritsy, "Ralph Hodgdon and Paul McMahon: Together 50 Years," *Bay Windows*, May 17, 2005.

"my friendship": Ellen Goodman, "Showing Us the Power of Marriage," *Boston Globe*, May 19, 2004.

"I'm so happy right now": Yvonne Abraham and Michael Paulson, "Wedding Day—First Gays Marry, Many Seek Licenses," *Boston Globe*, May 18, 2004.

a newspaper from Spain: Sasha Talcott, "Rush of Reporters

Worldwide Attracts Some Limelight, Too," *Boston Globe*, May 18, 2004.

"The legal case that will forever": Rev. William Sinkford quoted in Thomas Caywood, "Same-Sex Marriage: Married Goodridges Seal Case with Kiss," *Boston Herald*, May 18, 2004.

"By the power vested": Rev. Kim Crawford Harvie quoted in Rosenwald, "From This Day Paired for Life," *Boston Globe*, May 18, 2004.

"Ellen and I have waited": Maureen Brodoff and Josh Friedes quoted in Ethan Jacobs, "Four Who Fought for Marriage," *Bay Windows*, May 20, 2004.

"We figure after thirty-three years": Gloria Bailey quoted in Shelley Murphy and Jennifer Longley, "Some Couples Avoid 3-Day Wait to Wed," *Boston Globe*, May 18, 2004.

"Your Honor, I have been": Heidi and Perry Norton quoted in Norris Cavan, "Gay Weddings Make History—Couples across Bay State Exchange Vows under Law," *The Republican*, May 18, 2004.

"I believe we study history": Rev. Aaron Payson quoted in Linda Bock, "Northbridge Partners Tie Knot—Pioneering Pair Married in Joyful Church Service," *Worcester Telegram & Gazette*, May 18, 2004.

In the tiny rural town: Abraham and Paulson, "Wedding Day—First Gays Marry, Many Seek Licenses," *Boston Globe*, May 18, 2004.

Then Berman, Crawford Harvie: Ethan Jacobs, "A Week of Weddings," *Bay Windows*, May 27, 2004.

"I felt that my feet": Jennifer Hess, "Letter of Jennifer Hess," *One Year of Marriage Equality* (Boston: MassEquality, 2005), 51.

"was given birth for": Mary Bonauto quoted in Raphael Lewis, "Law Curbing Out-of-State Couples," *Boston Globe*, April 22, 2004.

"Someone should tell him": Arline Isaacson quoted in Yvonne Abraham and Frank Phillips, "Romney Eyes Order on Licenses—Seeks to Halt Marriages of Gay Outsiders," *Boston Globe*, May 19, 2004.

"If you're from": Joseph Curtatone quoted in Steve Marantz, "Same-Sex Marriage: Out-of-Staters File In," *Boston Herald*, May 18, 2004.

"SJC disagreed": The cases for two couples—one from Rhode Island and one from New York—were sent back to the lower court because their states had no express prohibitions on same-sex marriage.

As Tanya frantically called: Tanya McCloskey and Marcia Kadish, interview by authors, Cambridge, MA, April 26, 2006.

"We already felt married": Marion Kenneally, personal correspondence with authors, May 16, 2006.

"In that time of fear": Dawn Paul, "Letter of Dawn Paul," *One Year of Marriage Equality* (Boston: MassEquality, 2005), 56.

"Having a legal marriage": Steve Galante and Bill Pluckhahn, personal correspondence with authors, May 4, 2006.

"The United States does not": Julie Whitlow and Olga Merchan, interview with authors, Salem, MA, March 20, 2006.

"After seven years": Anne and Chad Gifford, "Our Family's Values," *Boston Globe*, May 17, 2005.

"On this Mother's Day":

Julian Baptista, "Thoughts on a Special Day," *Salem News*, May 12, 2006.

"Where do we find God?":
David O'Brien, "Does Love Matter?," *Boston Globe*, July 10, 2005.

CALL-OUTS

"It is the historic aspect":
Quoted in George Chauncey, *Why Marriage?* (New York: Basic Books, 2004), 143–144.

"The best part of being married":
John McDargh, "Letter of John McDargh," *One Year of Marriage Equality* (Boston: MassEquality, 2005), 158.

"When we leave this church":
Quoted in Yvonne Abraham, "Wedding Toast Poses Question for Travaglini," *Boston Globe*, November 23, 2004.

"Has our life changed":
George Smart, "Letter of George Smart," *One Year of Marriage Equality* (Boston: MassEquality, 2005), 137.

"When I looked in the eyes":
Quoted in Pam Belluck, "Massachusetts Rejects Bill to Eliminate Gay Marriage," *New York Times*, September 15, 2005.

"It's wonderful that we've been able to marry":
Quoted in Mary Jo Palumbo, "Gays Set to Mark Anniversary—Same Sex Weds under Fire a Year Later," *Boston Herald*, May 16, 2005.